FAT ★ FREE

FAT ★ FREE

amazing all-true adventures of
supersize woman!

JUDE MILNER

ILLUSTRATED BY
MARY WILSHIRE

JEREMY P. TARCHER/PENGUIN
A MEMBER OF PENGUIN GROUP (USA) INC.
NEW YORK

JEREMY P. TARCHER/PENGUIN
Published by the Penguin Group
Penguin Group (USA) Inc., 375 Hudson Street, New York, New York 10014, USA •
Penguin Group (Canada) 90 Eglinton Avenue East, Suite 700, Toronto, Ontario
M4P 2Y3, Canada (a division of Pearson Penguin Canada Inc.) • Penguin Books Ltd,
80 Strand, London WC2R 0RL, England • Penguin Ireland, 25 St Stephen's Green,
Dublin 2, Ireland (a division of Penguin Books Ltd) • Penguin Group (Australia),
250 Camberwell Road, Camberwell, Victoria 3124, Australia (a division of Pearson
Australia Group Pty Ltd) • Penguin Books India Pvt Ltd, 11 Community Centre,
Panchsheel Park, New Delhi–110 017, India • Penguin Group (NZ), Cnr Airborne
and Rosedale Roads, Albany, Auckland 1310, New Zealand (a division of Pearson New
Zealand Ltd) • Penguin Books (South Africa) (Pty) Ltd, 24 Sturdee Avenue,
Rosebank, Johannesburg 2196, South Africa

Penguin Books Ltd, Registered Offices:
80 Strand, London WC2R 0RL, England

Page 68 constitutes an extension of this copyright page.

Most Tarcher/Penguin books are available at special quantity discounts for bulk pur-
chase for sales promotions, premiums, fund-raising, and educational needs. Special
books or book excerpts also can be created to fit specific needs. For details, write
Penguin Group (USA) Inc. Special Markets, 375 Hudson Street, New York, NY 10014.

Library of Congress Cataloging-in-Publication Data

Milner, Jude, date.
Fat free : the amazing all-true adventures of supersize woman! / Jude Milner.
            p.   cm.
            ISBN 1-58542-501-X
1. Milner, Jude, 1953—Health—Comic books, strips, etc.   2. Overweight
women—United States—Biography—Comic books, strips, etc.   I. Title.
    RC552.O25M57   2006   2005055546
            362.196'3980092—dc22

Printed in the United States of America

1   3   5   7   9   10   8   6   4   2

This book is printed on acid-free paper. ∞

BOOK DESIGN BY STEPHANIE HUNTWORK

While the author has made every effort to provide accurate telephone numbers and
Internet addresses at the time of publication, neither the publisher nor the author
assumes any responsibility for errors, or for changes that occur after publication.
Further, the publisher does not have any control over and does not assume any
responsibility for author or third-party websites or their content.

For Mom,
who lives her life
with inspiring courage

a note on the art

Art Director James Sherman chose to give this book a very different look and feel than most graphic novels.

Traditionally, comics and graphic novels begin with pencil sketches that are later worked over by an inker, who defines and thickens the lines. Increasingly, high-tech imaging techniques that rely on electronic tools have redefined the medium.

Rather than aiming for either a traditional comic book or a computer graphics style, however, Sherman asked Mary Wilshire to produce unadorned pencil renderings, modified only by an eraser. His innovative, return-to-basics direction posed a formidable challenge to the artist.

As the reader can see, Wilshire succeeded in surpassing expectations with the 349 original pencil drawings that comprise this book. Some have been brought to a very detailed "finished" state, while others are minimally sketched. The result is a mosaic in varying shades of emotional intensity. Wilshire's drawings masterfully capture the body language, gestures, and facial expressions of the author at every age, weight, and emotion. They have a life of their own that goes far beyond visual storytelling.

The result is a fitting counterpoint to Jude Milner's honest, painful, and funny account of her lifelong battles with her body. In some of the drawings, one can even see the variations and sequences of the pencil meeting the paper. Thus, the reader can follow not only Jude's story but the sweep, wit, and truth of Wilshire's pencil.

—*Richard Milner*

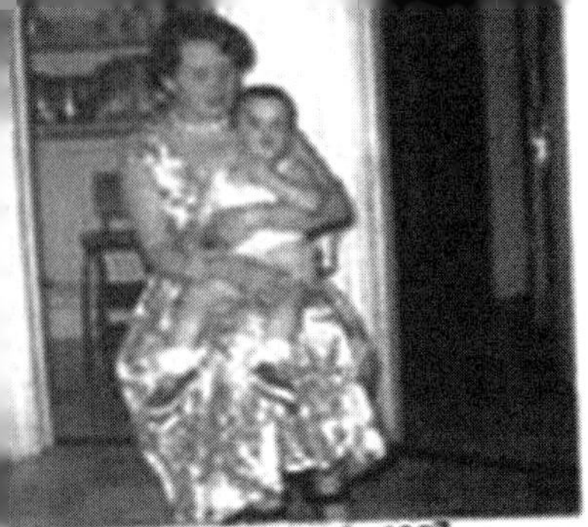

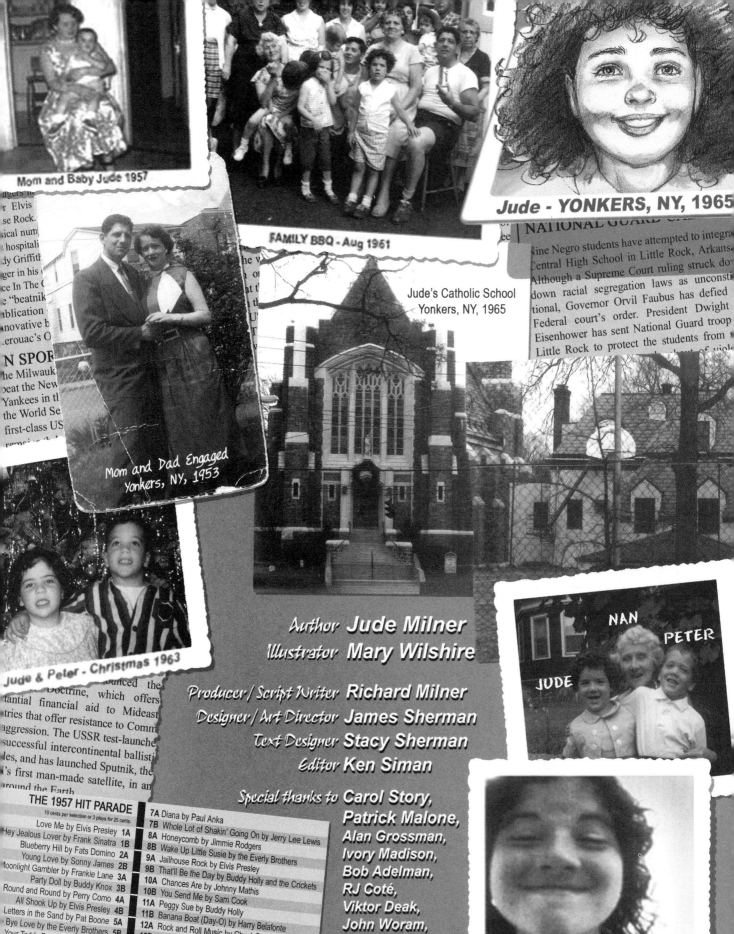

Mom and Baby Jude 1957

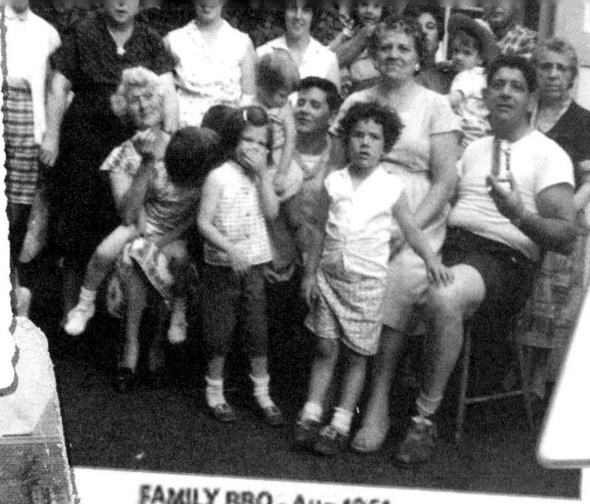

FAMILY BBQ - Aug 1961

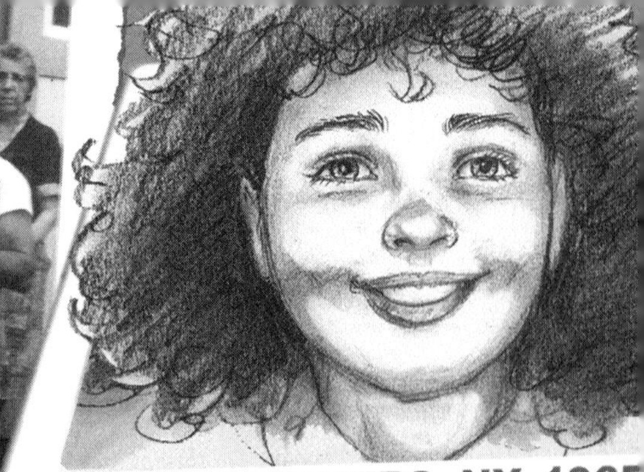

Jude - YONKERS, NY, 1965

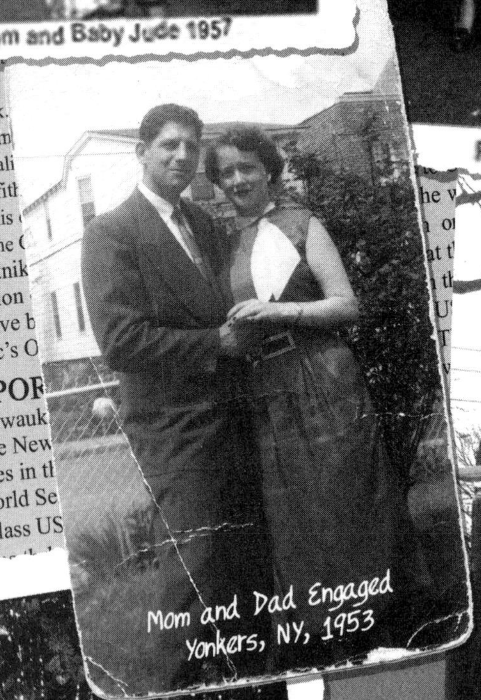

Mom and Dad Engaged
Yonkers, NY, 1953

agers ...
r Elvis
se Rock.
sical num
hospitali
dy Griffith
ger in his
ce In The C
"beatnik
ublication
nnovative b
Kerouac's O

N SPOR
he Milwauk
beat the New
Yankees in th
the World Se
first-class US

NATIONAL GUARD ...

Nine Negro students have attempted to integra
Central High School in Little Rock, Arkans.
Although a Supreme Court ruling struck do
down racial segregation laws as unconsti
tional, Governor Orvil Faubus has defied
Federal court's order. President Dwight
Eisenhower has sent National Guard troop
Little Rock to protect the students from

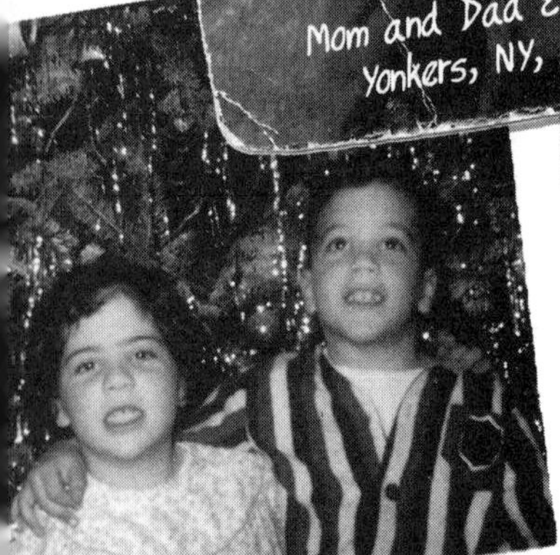

Jude & Peter - Christmas 1963

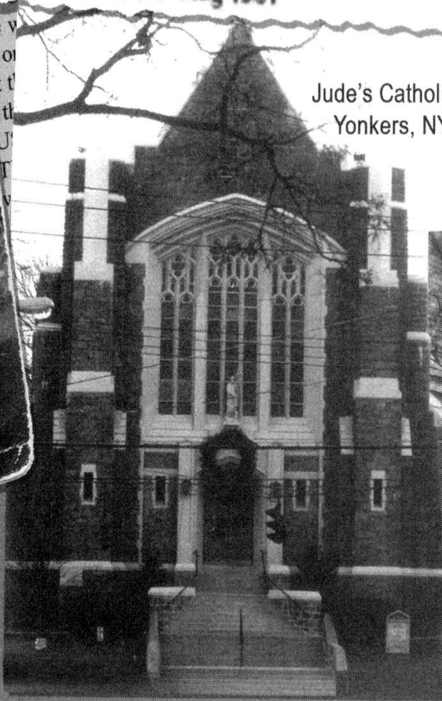

Jude's Catholic School
Yonkers, NY, 1965

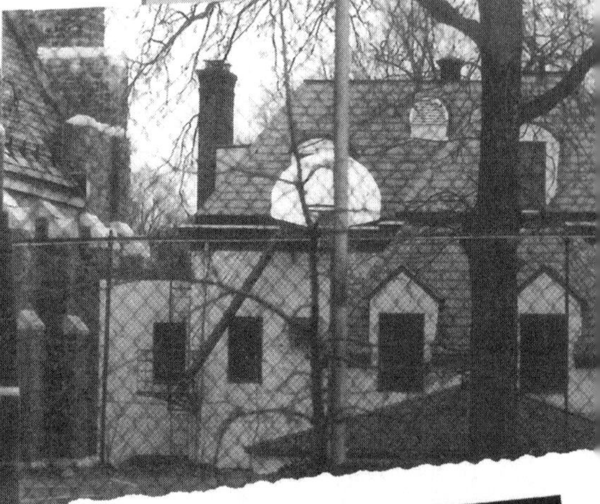

...nounced the ... Doctrine, which offers ...tantial financial aid to Mideast ...tries that offer resistance to Comm... aggression. The USSR test-launche... successful intercontinental ballisti... les, and has launched Sputnik, the ...'s first man-made satellite, in an ...round the Earth.

Author **Jude Milner**
Illustrator **Mary Wilshire**

Producer / Script Writer **Richard Milner**
Designer / Art Director **James Sherman**
Text Designer **Stacy Sherman**
Editor **Ken Siman**

Special thanks to **Carol Story, Patrick Malone, Alan Grossman, Ivory Madison, Bob Adelman, RJ Coté, Viktor Deak, John Woram, Pete Von Sholly, and Dave Stone**

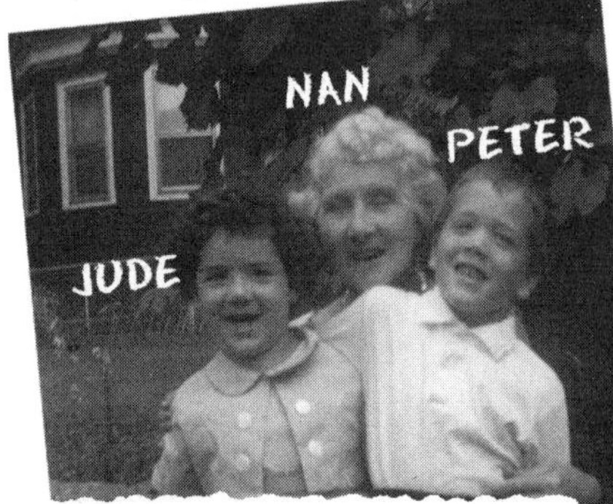

NAN
PETER
JUDE

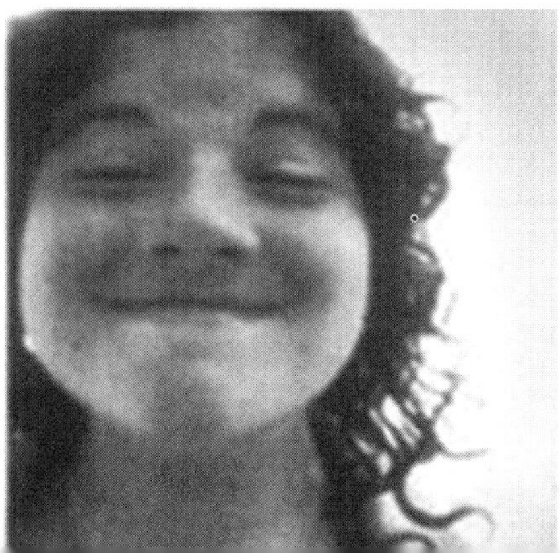

THE 1957 HIT PARADE

10 cents per selection or 3 plays for 25 cents.

Love Me by Elvis Presley	1A	7A	Diana by Paul Anka
Hey Jealous Lover by Frank Sinatra	1B	7B	Whole Lot of Shakin' Going On by Jerry Lee Lewis
Blueberry Hill by Fats Domino	2A	8A	Honeycomb by Jimmie Rodgers
Young Love by Sonny James	2B	8B	Wake Up Little Susie by the Everly Brothers
Moonlight Gambler by Frankie Lane	3A	9A	Jailhouse Rock by Elvis Presley
Party Doll by Buddy Knox	3B	9B	That'll Be the Day by Buddy Holly and the Crickets
Round and Round by Perry Como	4A	10A	Chances Are by Johnny Mathis
All Shook Up by Elvis Presley	4B	10B	You Send Me by Sam Cook
Letters in the Sand by Pat Boone	5A	11A	Peggy Sue by Buddy Holly
Bye Love by the Everly Brothers	5B	11B	Banana Boat (Day-O) by Harry Belafonte
Your Teddy Bear by Elvis Presley	6A	12A	Rock and Roll Music by Chuck Berry
Tammy by Debbie Reynolds	6B	12B	I'm Walkin' by Fats Domino
		13A	Twelfth of Never by Johnny Mathis
		13B	Wonderful, Wonderful by Johnny Mathis

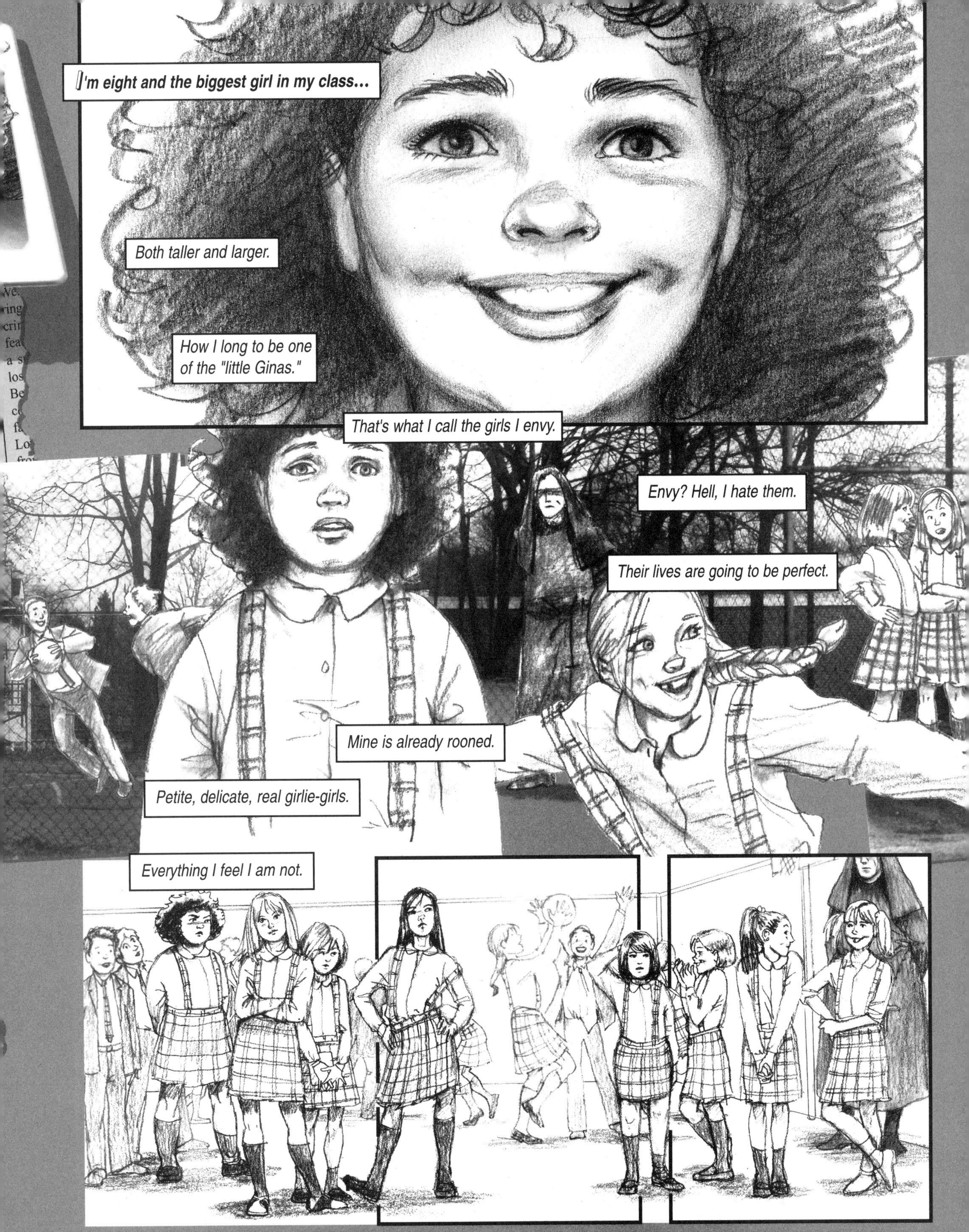
I'm eight and the biggest girl in my class...
Both taller and larger.
How I long to be one of the "little Ginas."
That's what I call the girls I envy.
Envy? Hell, I hate them.
Their lives are going to be perfect.
Mine is already rooned.
Petite, delicate, real girlie-girls.
Everything I feel I am not.

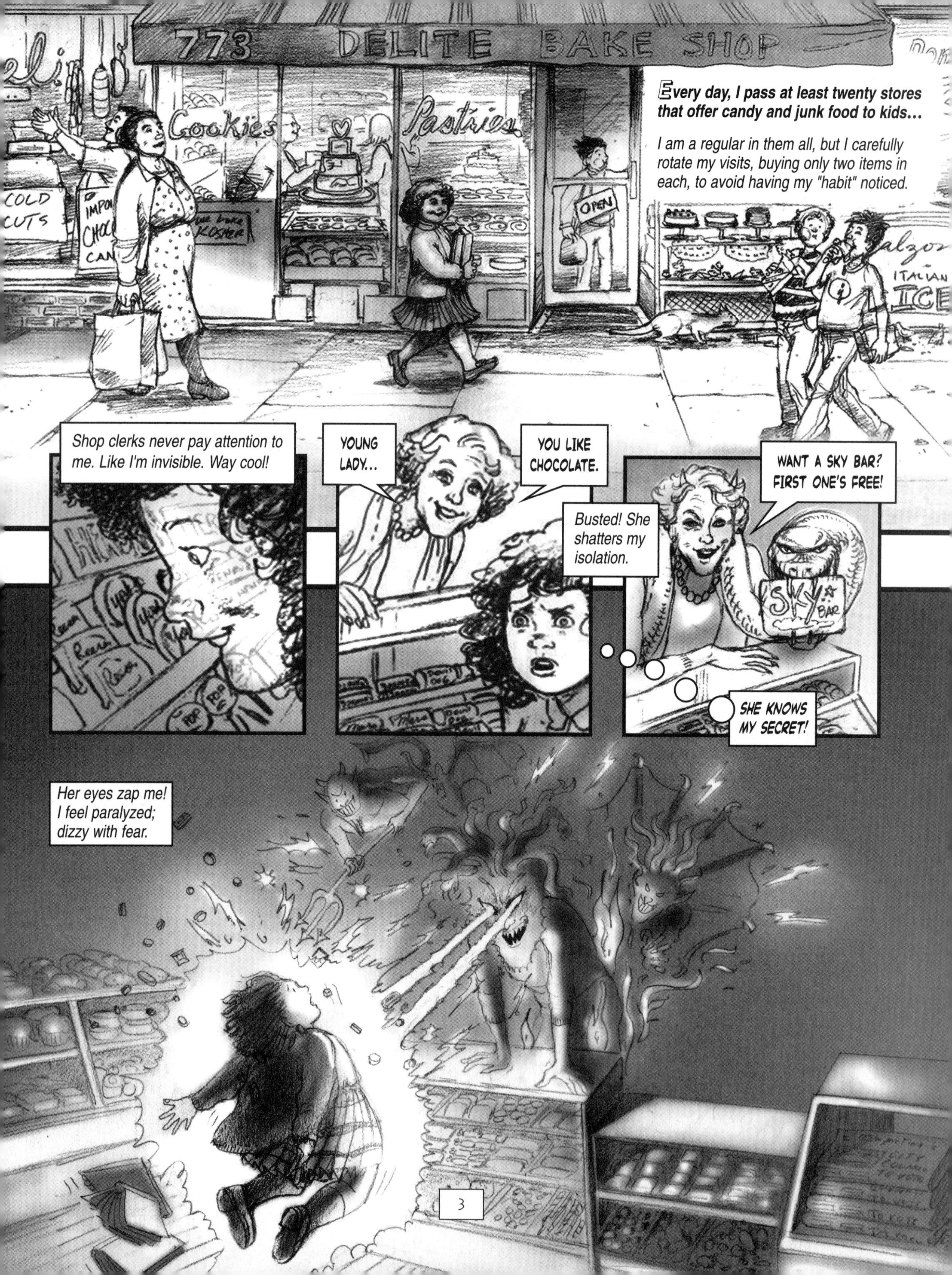

773 DELITE BAKE SHOP
Every day, I pass at least twenty stores that offer candy and junk food to kids…
I am a regular in them all, but I carefully rotate my visits, buying only two items in each, to avoid having my "habit" noticed.
Cookies
Pastries
COLD CUTS
We bake KOSHER
OPEN
ITALIAN ICE
Shop clerks never pay attention to me. Like I'm invisible. Way cool!
YOUNG LADY…
YOU LIKE CHOCOLATE.
Busted! She shatters my isolation.
WANT A SKY BAR? FIRST ONE'S FREE!
SKY BAR
SHE KNOWS MY SECRET!
Her eyes zap me! I feel paralyzed; dizzy with fear.

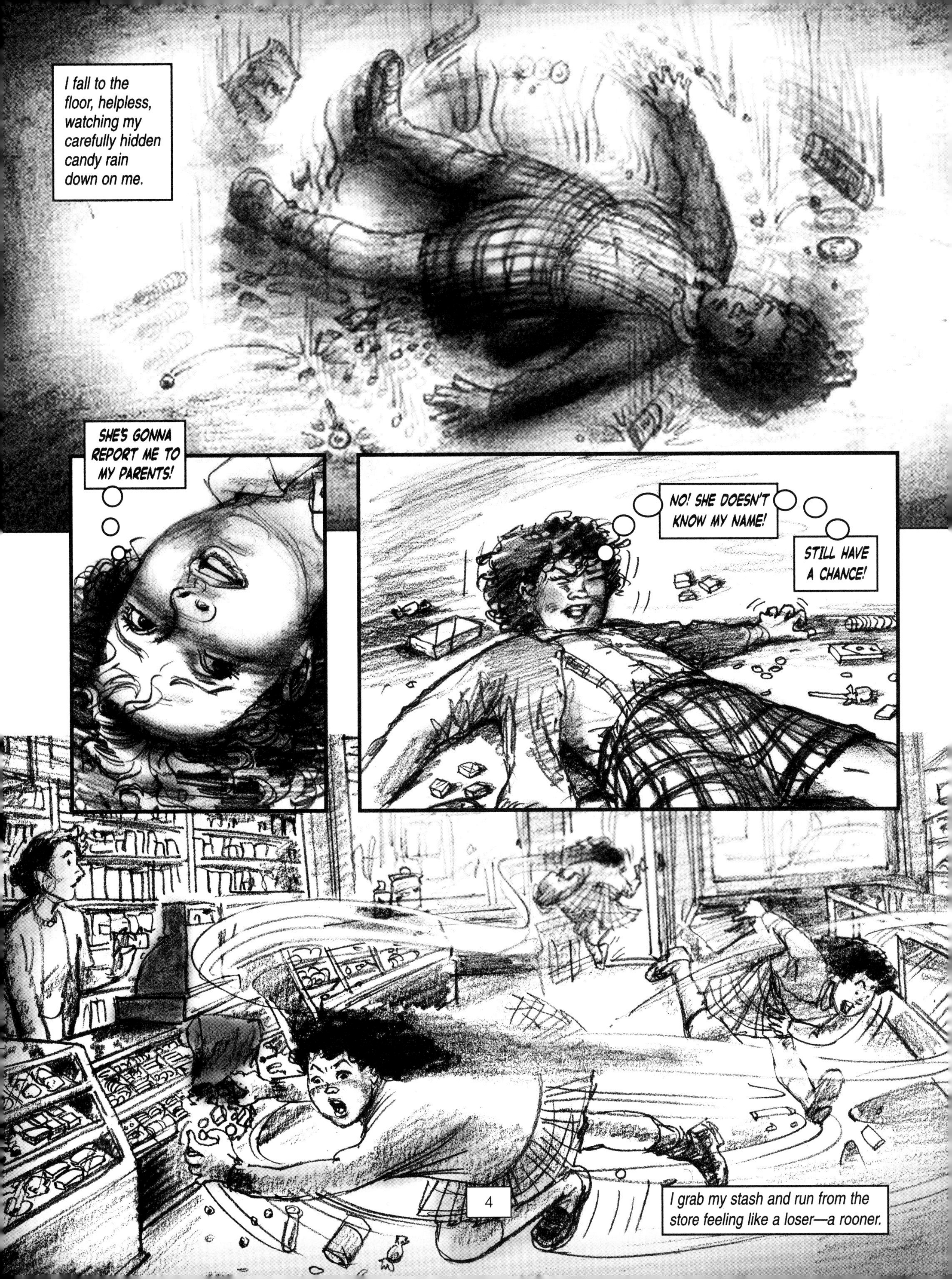
I fall to the floor, helpless, watching my carefully hidden candy rain down on me.
SHE'S GONNA REPORT ME TO MY PARENTS!
NO! SHE DOESN'T KNOW MY NAME!
STILL HAVE A CHANCE!
I grab my stash and run from the store feeling like a loser—a rooner.

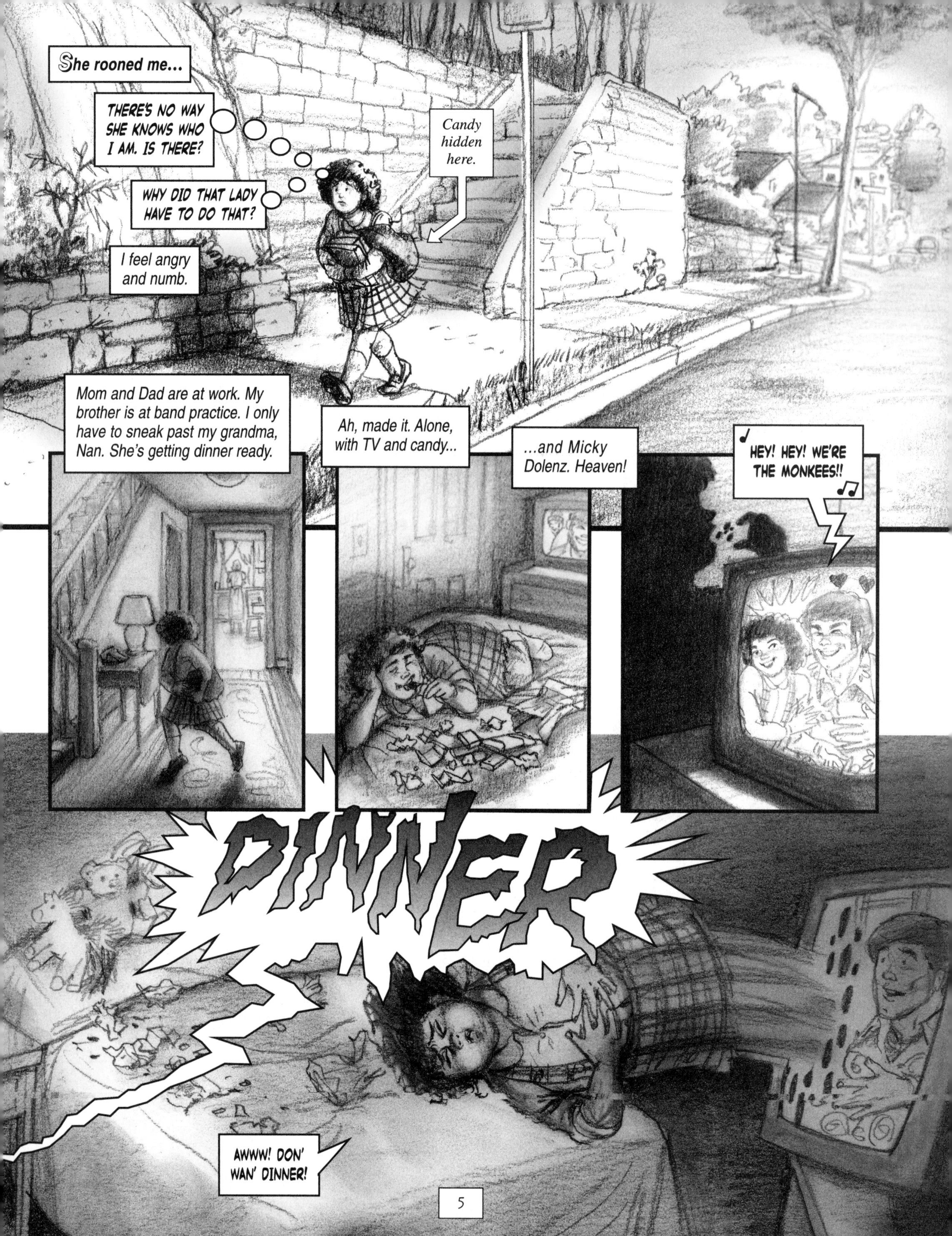
She rooned me...
THERE'S NO WAY SHE KNOWS WHO I AM. IS THERE?
WHY DID THAT LADY HAVE TO DO THAT?
I feel angry and numb.
Candy hidden here.
Mom and Dad are at work. My brother is at band practice. I only have to sneak past my grandma, Nan. She's getting dinner ready.
Ah, made it. Alone, with TV and candy...
...and Micky Dolenz. Heaven!
HEY! HEY! WE'RE THE MONKEES!!
DINNER
AWWW! DON' WAN' DINNER!

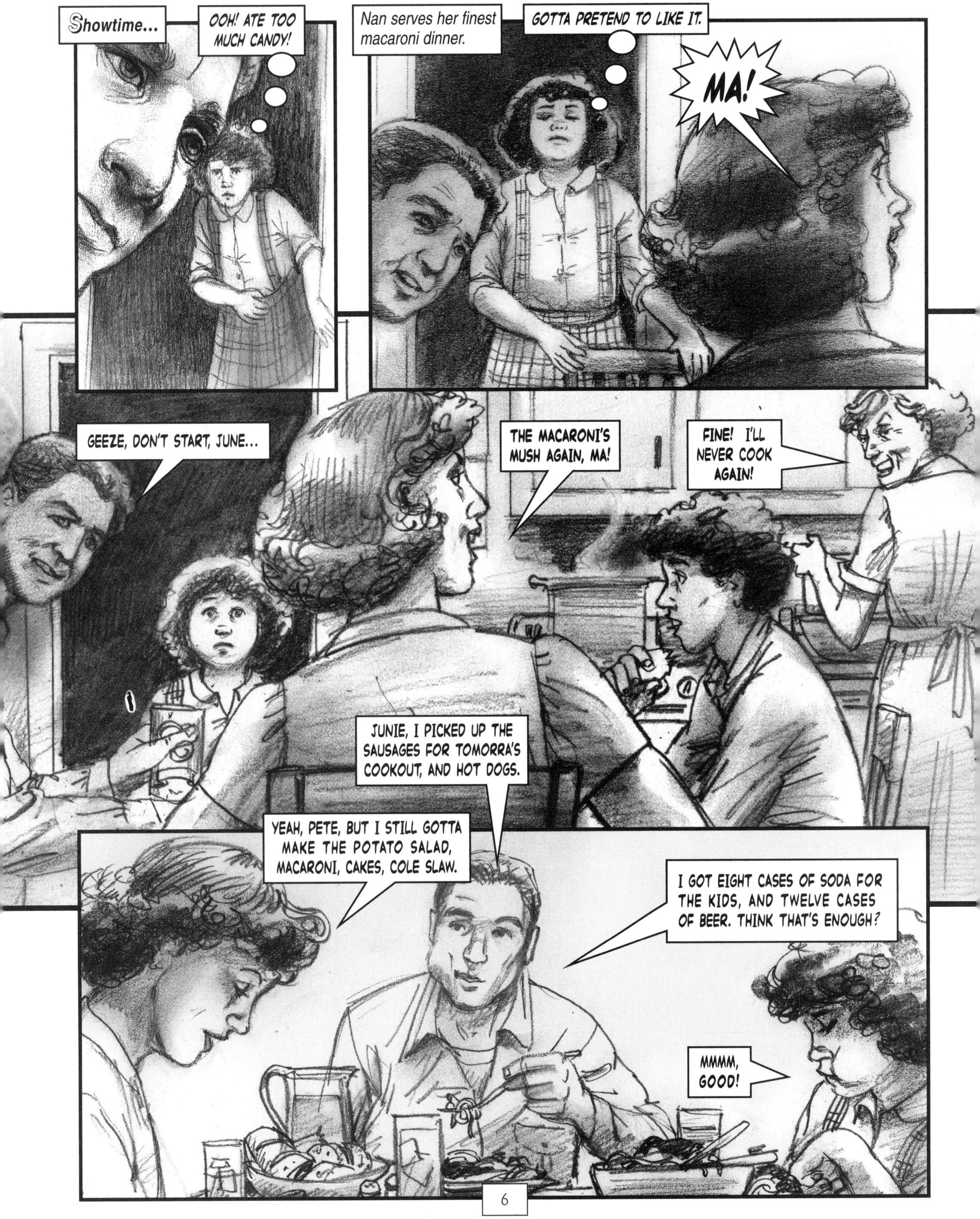

Showtime...
OOH! ATE TOO MUCH CANDY!
Nan serves her finest macaroni dinner.
GOTTA PRETEND TO LIKE IT.
MA!
GEEZE, DON'T START, JUNE...
THE MACARONI'S MUSH AGAIN, MA!
FINE! I'LL NEVER COOK AGAIN!
JUNIE, I PICKED UP THE SAUSAGES FOR TOMORRA'S COOKOUT, AND HOT DOGS.
YEAH, PETE, BUT I STILL GOTTA MAKE THE POTATO SALAD, MACARONI, CAKES, COLE SLAW.
I GOT EIGHT CASES OF SODA FOR THE KIDS, AND TWELVE CASES OF BEER. THINK THAT'S ENOUGH?
MMMM, GOOD!

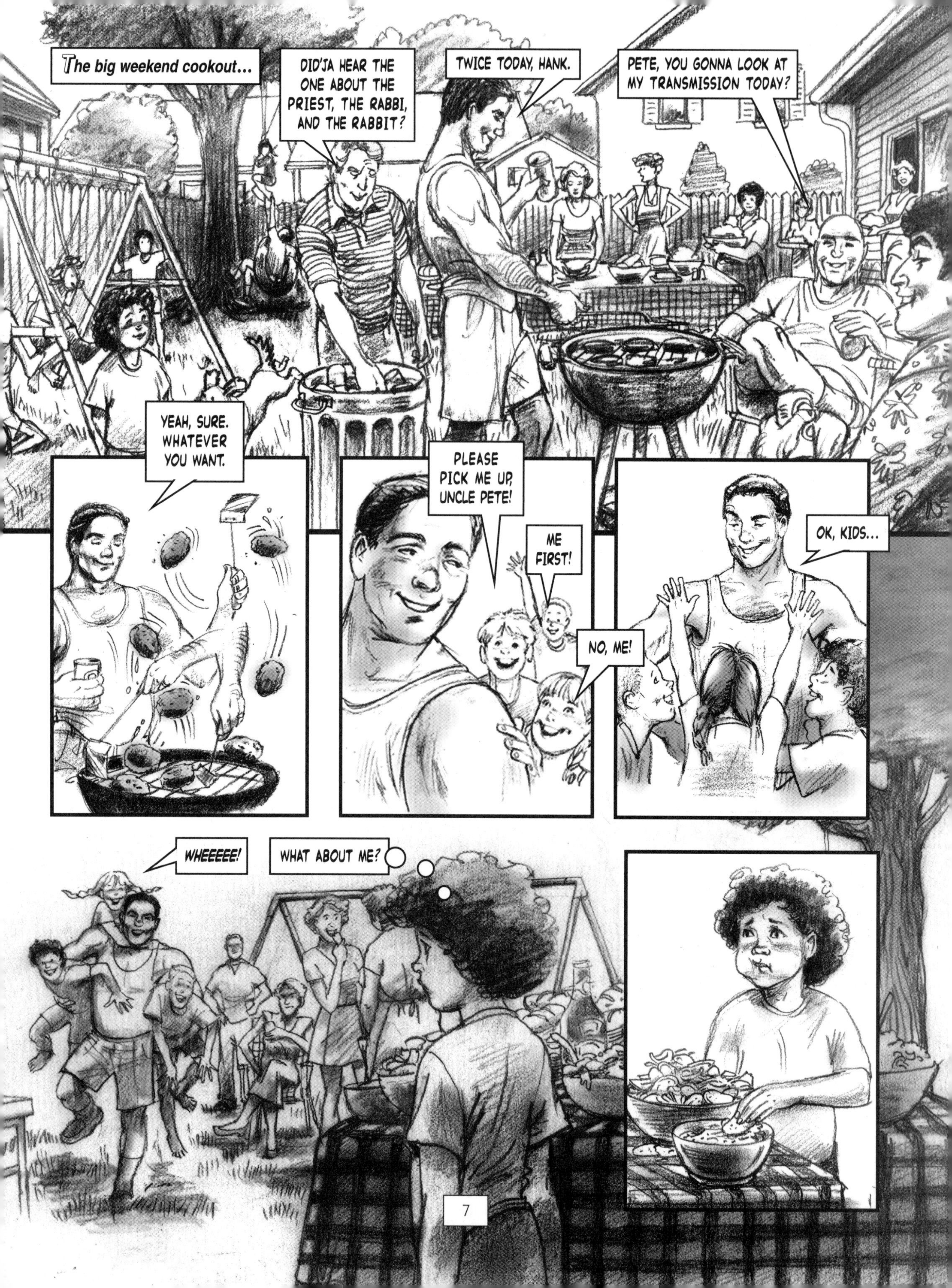
The big weekend cookout...
DID'JA HEAR THE ONE ABOUT THE PRIEST, THE RABBI, AND THE RABBIT?
TWICE TODAY, HANK.
PETE, YOU GONNA LOOK AT MY TRANSMISSION TODAY?
YEAH, SURE. WHATEVER YOU WANT.
PLEASE PICK ME UP, UNCLE PETE!
ME FIRST!
NO, ME!
OK, KIDS...
WHEEEEE!
WHAT ABOUT ME?

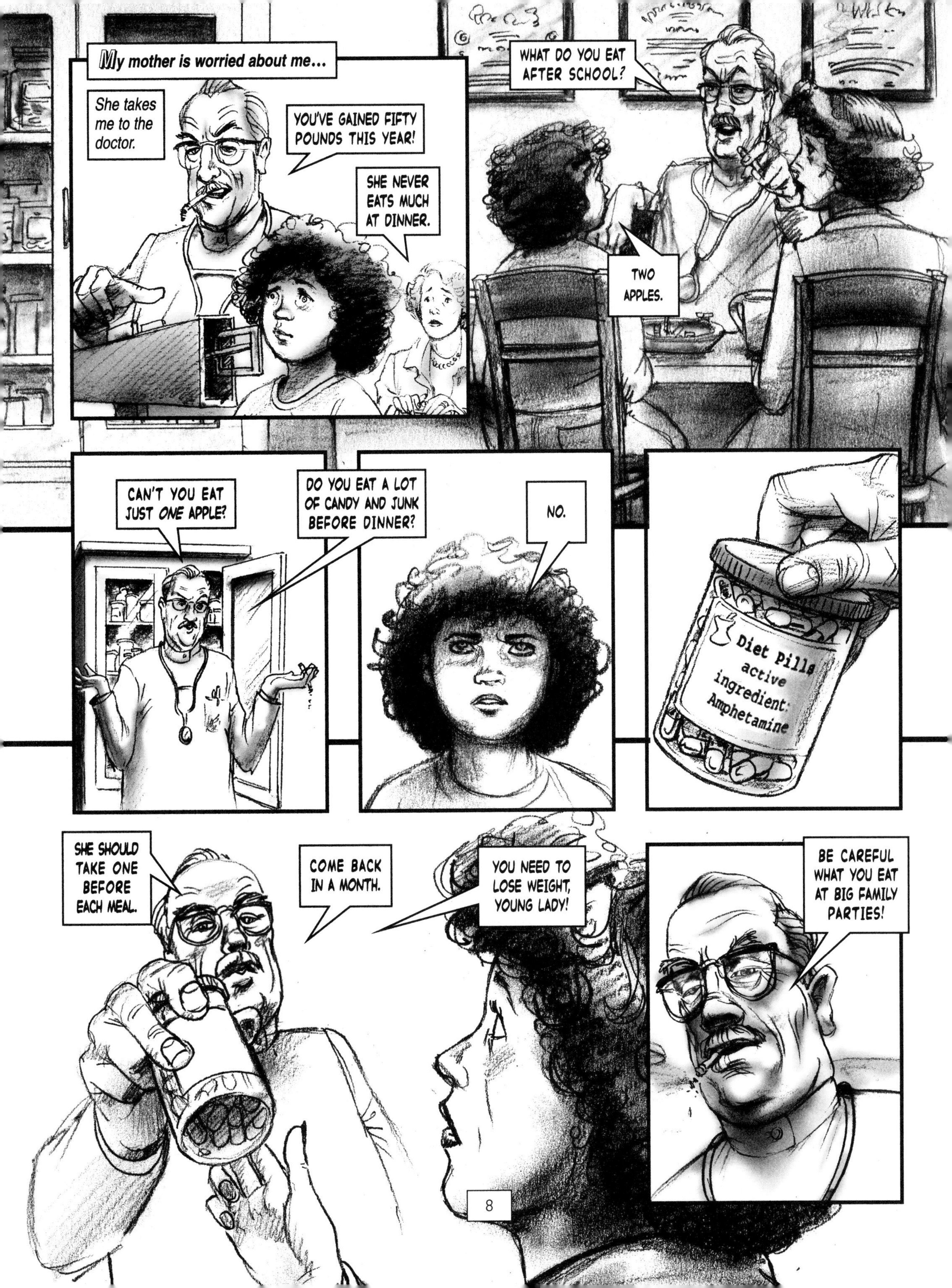
My mother is worried about me...
She takes me to the doctor.
YOU'VE GAINED FIFTY POUNDS THIS YEAR!
SHE NEVER EATS MUCH AT DINNER.
WHAT DO YOU EAT AFTER SCHOOL?
TWO APPLES.
CAN'T YOU EAT JUST ONE APPLE?
DO YOU EAT A LOT OF CANDY AND JUNK BEFORE DINNER?
NO.
Diet Pills active ingredient: Amphetamine
SHE SHOULD TAKE ONE BEFORE EACH MEAL.
COME BACK IN A MONTH.
YOU NEED TO LOSE WEIGHT, YOUNG LADY!
BE CAREFUL WHAT YOU EAT AT BIG FAMILY PARTIES!

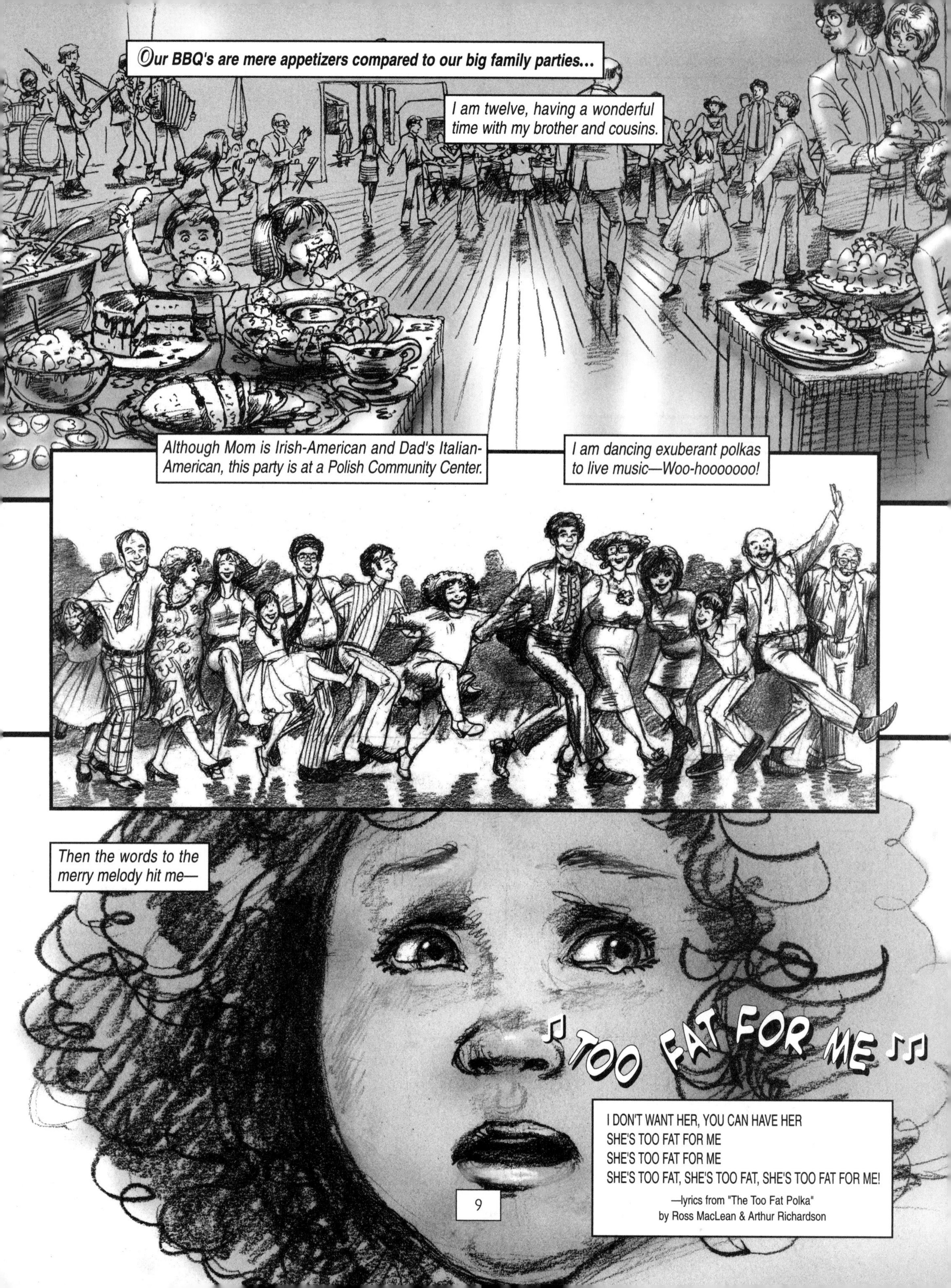
Our BBQ's are mere appetizers compared to our big family parties...
I am twelve, having a wonderful time with my brother and cousins.
Although Mom is Irish-American and Dad's Italian-American, this party is at a Polish Community Center.
I am dancing exuberant polkas to live music—Woo-hoooooo!
Then the words to the merry melody hit me—
♫ TOO FAT FOR ME ♫♫
I DON'T WANT HER, YOU CAN HAVE HER
SHE'S TOO FAT FOR ME
SHE'S TOO FAT FOR ME
SHE'S TOO FAT, SHE'S TOO FAT, SHE'S TOO FAT FOR ME!
—lyrics from "The Too Fat Polka"
by Ross MacLean & Arthur Richardson

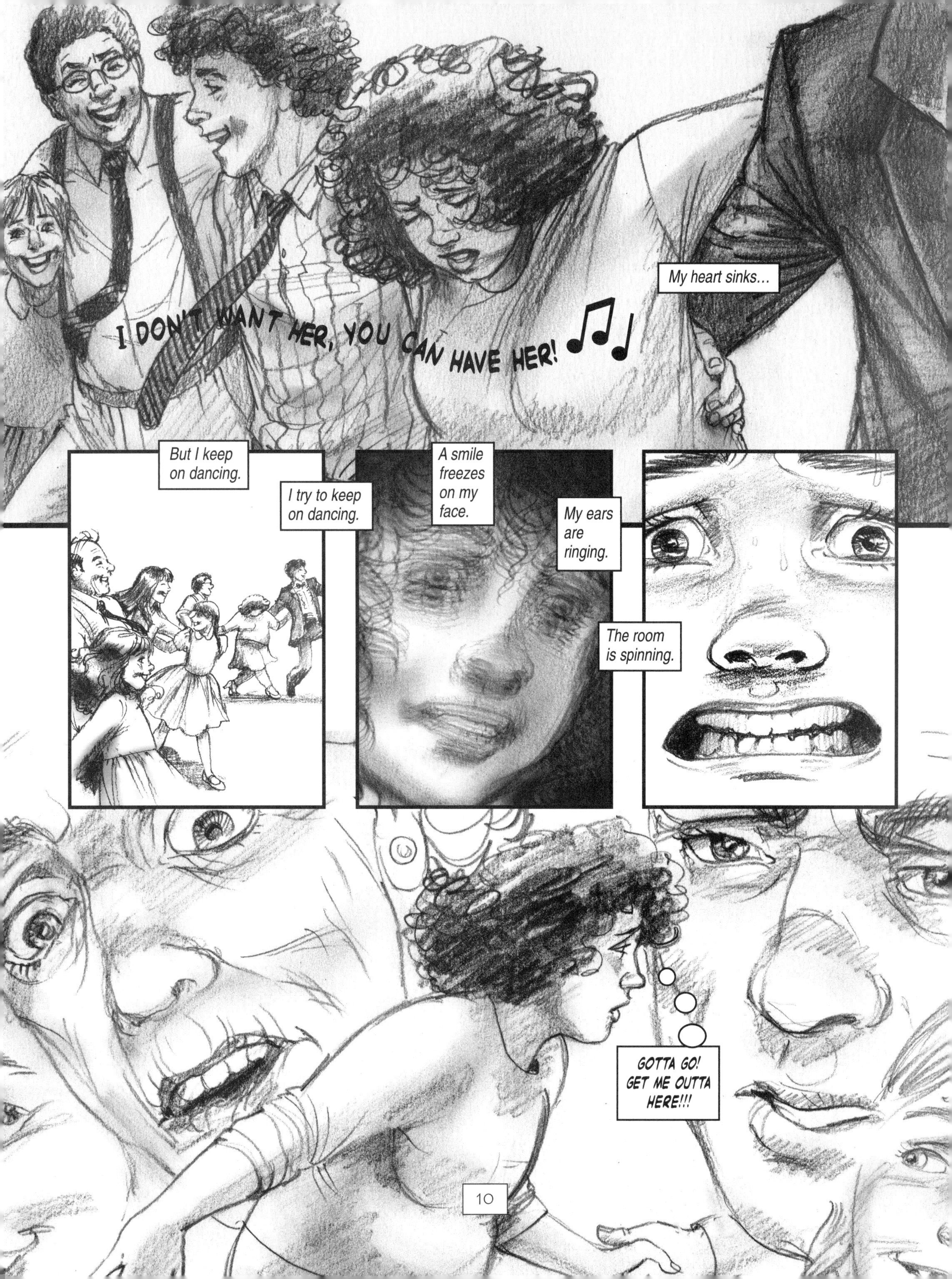
I DON'T WANT HER, YOU CAN HAVE HER! ♫♩
My heart sinks…
But I keep on dancing.
I try to keep on dancing.
A smile freezes on my face.
My ears are ringing.
The room is spinning.
GOTTA GO! GET ME OUTTA HERE!!!

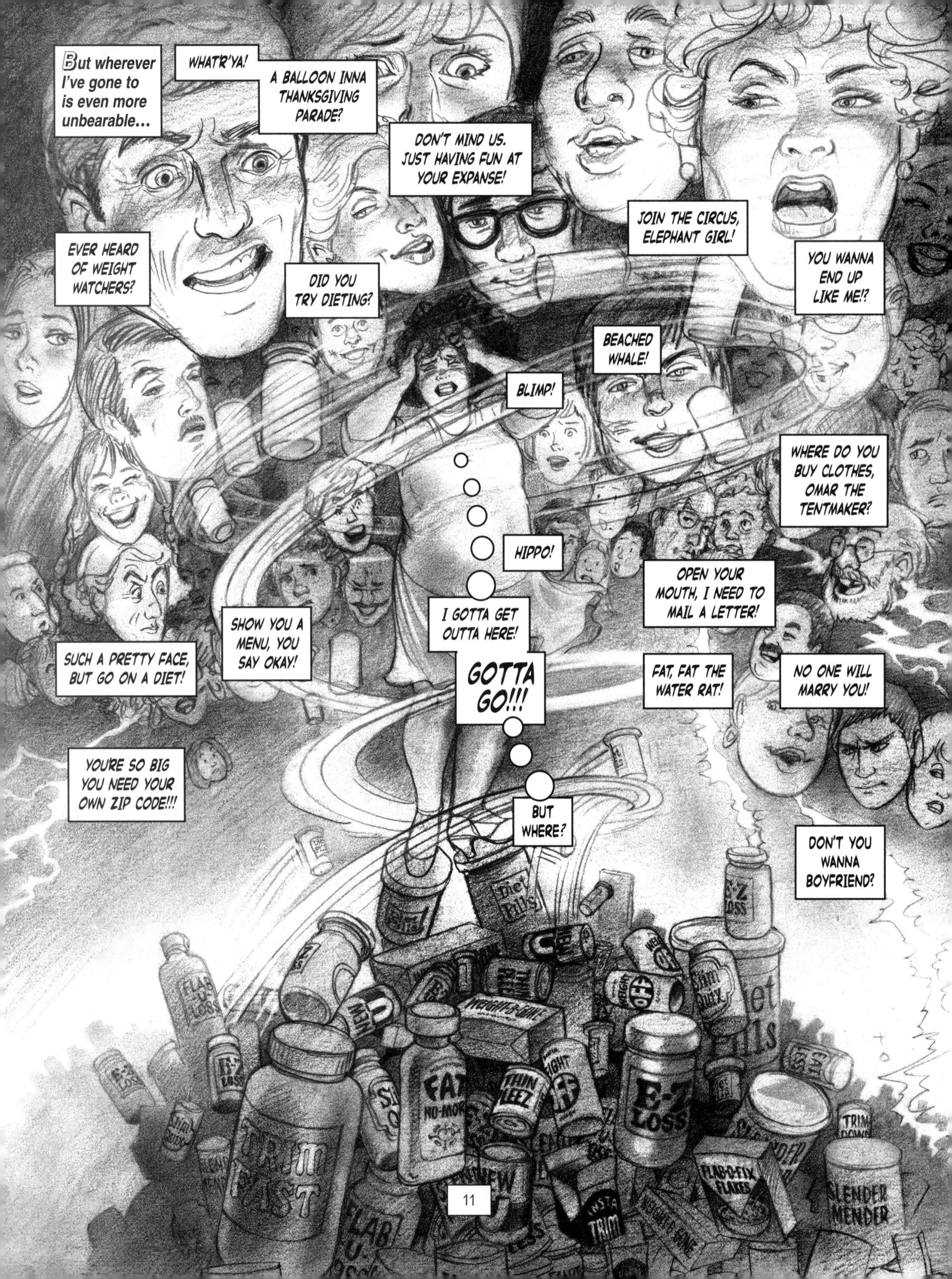
But wherever I've gone to is even more unbearable…
WHAT'R'YA!
A BALLOON INNA THANKSGIVING PARADE?
DON'T MIND US. JUST HAVING FUN AT YOUR EXPANSE!
JOIN THE CIRCUS, ELEPHANT GIRL!
EVER HEARD OF WEIGHT WATCHERS?
DID YOU TRY DIETING?
YOU WANNA END UP LIKE ME!?
BEACHED WHALE!
BLIMP!
WHERE DO YOU BUY CLOTHES, OMAR THE TENTMAKER?
HIPPO!
OPEN YOUR MOUTH, I NEED TO MAIL A LETTER!
SHOW YOU A MENU, YOU SAY OKAY!
I GOTTA GET OUTTA HERE!
SUCH A PRETTY FACE, BUT GO ON A DIET!
GOTTA GO!!!
FAT, FAT THE WATER RAT!
NO ONE WILL MARRY YOU!
YOU'RE SO BIG YOU NEED YOUR OWN ZIP CODE!!!
BUT WHERE?
DON'T YOU WANNA BOYFRIEND?
Diet Pills
E-Z LOSS
FLAB-U-LOSS
FAT NO-MORE
THIN LEEZ
TRIM FAST
FLAB-O-FIX FLAKES
SLENDER MENDER
INSTA TRIM
WEIGHT-B-GONE

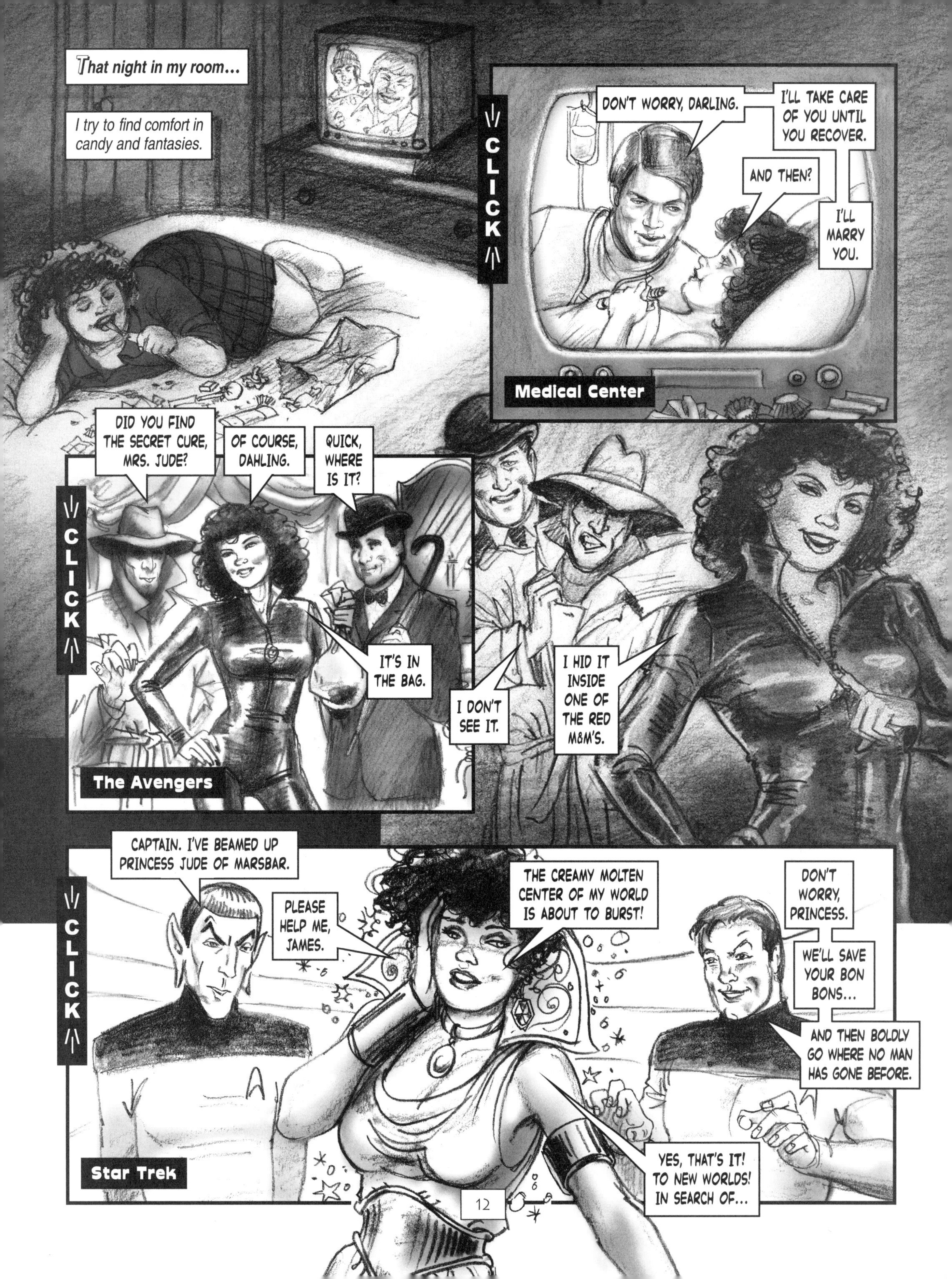
That night in my room...
I try to find comfort in candy and fantasies.
CLICK
DON'T WORRY, DARLING.
I'LL TAKE CARE OF YOU UNTIL YOU RECOVER.
AND THEN?
I'LL MARRY YOU.
Medical Center
CLICK
DID YOU FIND THE SECRET CURE, MRS. JUDE?
OF COURSE, DAHLING.
QUICK, WHERE IS IT?
IT'S IN THE BAG.
I DON'T SEE IT.
I HID IT INSIDE ONE OF THE RED M&M'S.
The Avengers
CLICK
CAPTAIN. I'VE BEAMED UP PRINCESS JUDE OF MARSBAR.
PLEASE HELP ME, JAMES.
THE CREAMY MOLTEN CENTER OF MY WORLD IS ABOUT TO BURST!
DON'T WORRY, PRINCESS.
WE'LL SAVE YOUR BON BONS...
AND THEN BOLDLY GO WHERE NO MAN HAS GONE BEFORE.
YES, THAT'S IT! TO NEW WORLDS! IN SEARCH OF...
Star Trek

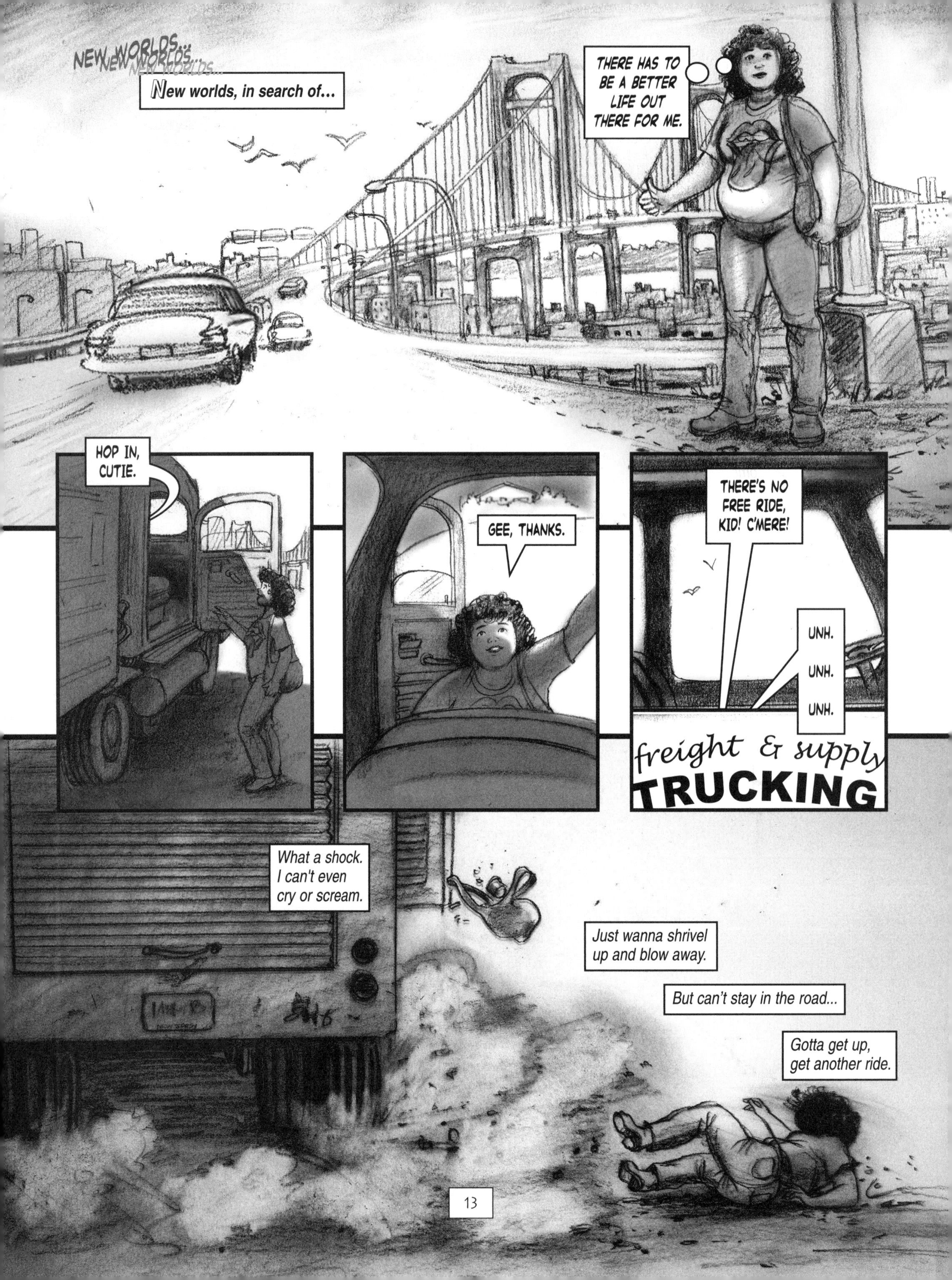
NEW WORLDS...
NEW WORLDS...
NEW WORLDS...
New worlds, in search of...
THERE HAS TO BE A BETTER LIFE OUT THERE FOR ME.
HOP IN, CUTIE.
GEE, THANKS.
THERE'S NO FREE RIDE, KID! C'MERE!
UNH.
UNH.
UNH.
freight & supply
TRUCKING
What a shock. I can't even cry or scream.
Just wanna shrivel up and blow away.
But can't stay in the road...
Gotta get up, get another ride.

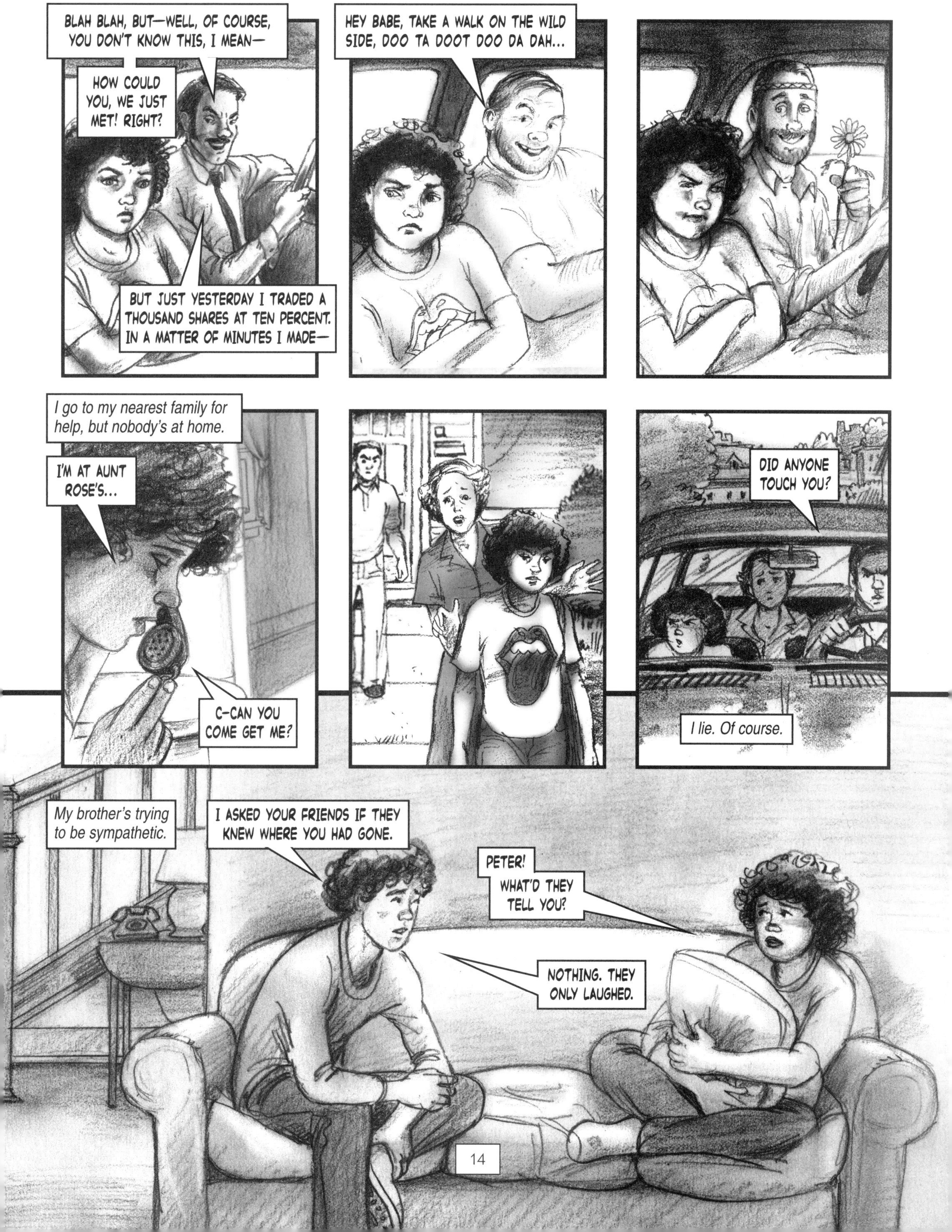

BLAH BLAH, BUT—WELL, OF COURSE, YOU DON'T KNOW THIS, I MEAN—
HOW COULD YOU, WE JUST MET! RIGHT?
BUT JUST YESTERDAY I TRADED A THOUSAND SHARES AT TEN PERCENT. IN A MATTER OF MINUTES I MADE—
HEY BABE, TAKE A WALK ON THE WILD SIDE, DOO TA DOOT DOO DA DAH...
I go to my nearest family for help, but nobody's at home.
I'M AT AUNT ROSE'S...
C-CAN YOU COME GET ME?
DID ANYONE TOUCH YOU?
I lie. Of course.
My brother's trying to be sympathetic.
I ASKED YOUR FRIENDS IF THEY KNEW WHERE YOU HAD GONE.
PETER!
WHAT'D THEY TELL YOU?
NOTHING. THEY ONLY LAUGHED.

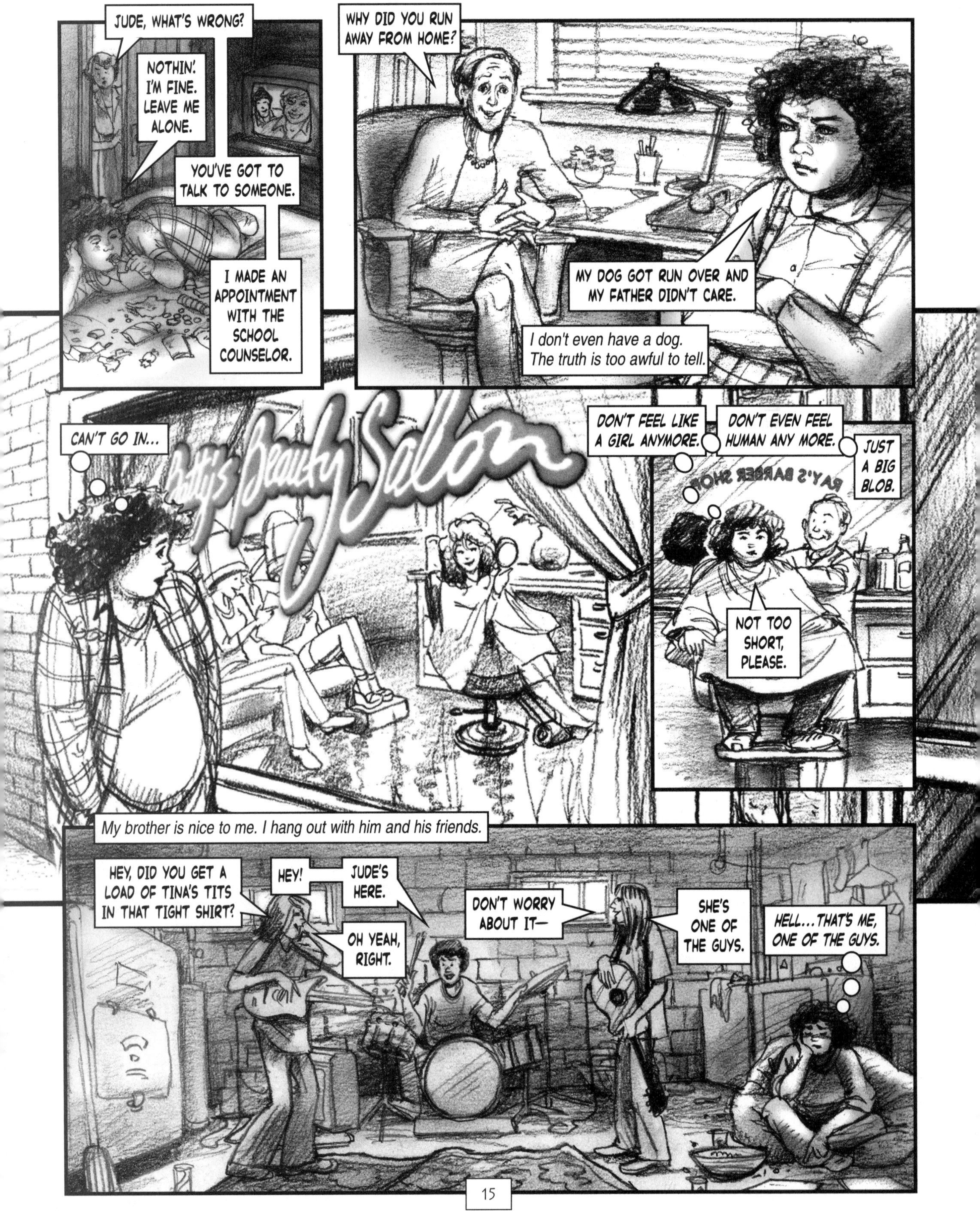
JUDE, WHAT'S WRONG?
NOTHIN'. I'M FINE. LEAVE ME ALONE.
YOU'VE GOT TO TALK TO SOMEONE.
I MADE AN APPOINTMENT WITH THE SCHOOL COUNSELOR.
WHY DID YOU RUN AWAY FROM HOME?
MY DOG GOT RUN OVER AND MY FATHER DIDN'T CARE.
I don't even have a dog. The truth is too awful to tell.
CAN'T GO IN...
Patty's Beauty Salon
DON'T FEEL LIKE A GIRL ANYMORE.
DON'T EVEN FEEL HUMAN ANY MORE.
JUST A BIG BLOB.
RAY'S BARBER SHOP
NOT TOO SHORT, PLEASE.
My brother is nice to me. I hang out with him and his friends.
HEY, DID YOU GET A LOAD OF TINA'S TITS IN THAT TIGHT SHIRT?
HEY!
JUDE'S HERE.
OH YEAH, RIGHT.
DON'T WORRY ABOUT IT—
SHE'S ONE OF THE GUYS.
HELL...THAT'S ME, ONE OF THE GUYS.

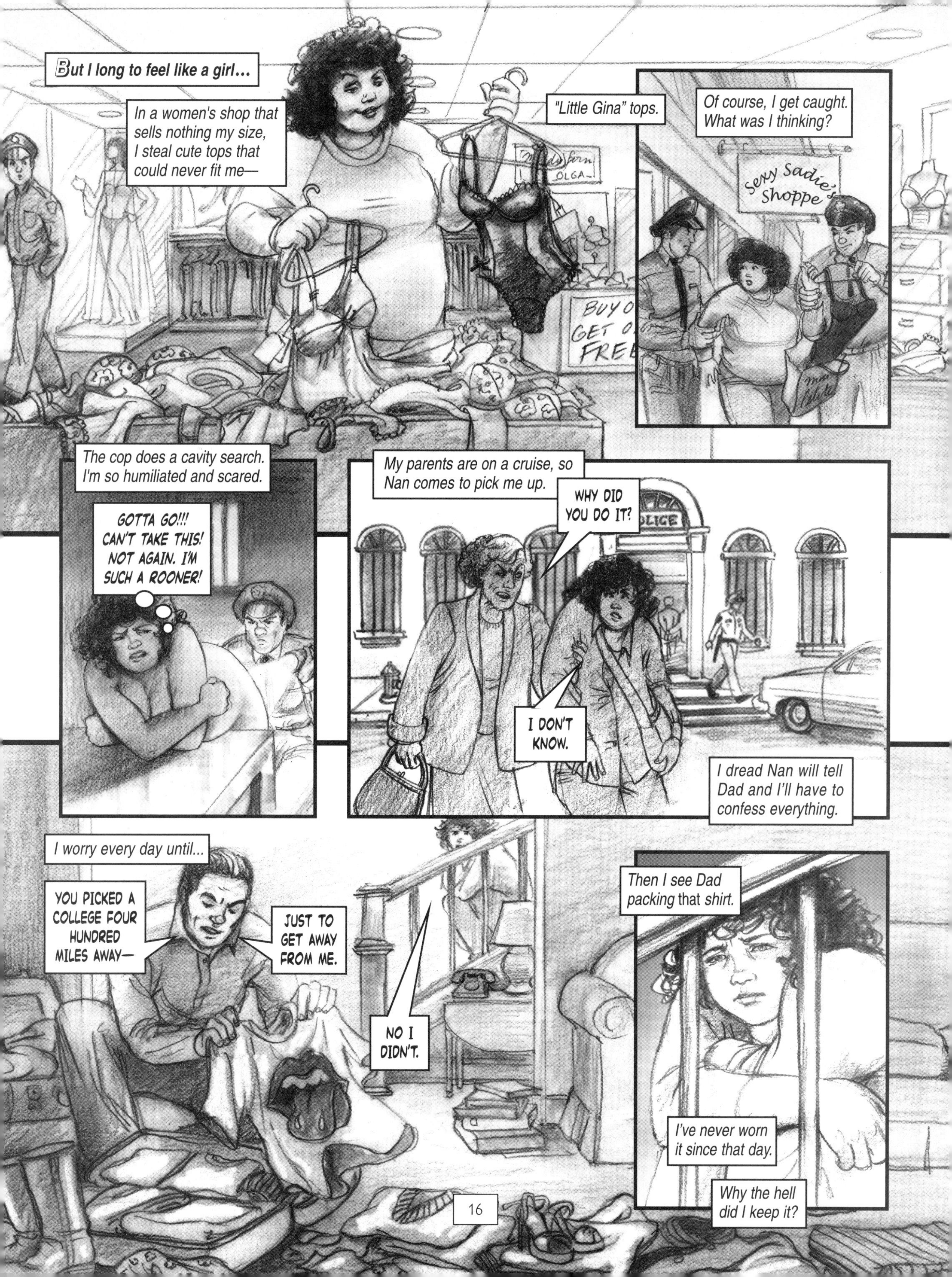
But I long to feel like a girl…
In a women's shop that sells nothing my size, I steal cute tops that could never fit me—
"Little Gina" tops.
OLGA
BUY O
GET O
FREE
Of course, I get caught. What was I thinking?
Sexy Sadie's Shoppe
The cop does a cavity search. I'm so humiliated and scared.
GOTTA GO!!! CAN'T TAKE THIS! NOT AGAIN. I'M SUCH A ROONER!
My parents are on a cruise, so Nan comes to pick me up.
WHY DID YOU DO IT?
OLICE
I DON'T KNOW.
I dread Nan will tell Dad and I'll have to confess everything.
I worry every day until…
YOU PICKED A COLLEGE FOUR HUNDRED MILES AWAY—
JUST TO GET AWAY FROM ME.
NO I DIDN'T.
Then I see Dad packing that shirt.
I've never worn it since that day.
Why the hell did I keep it?

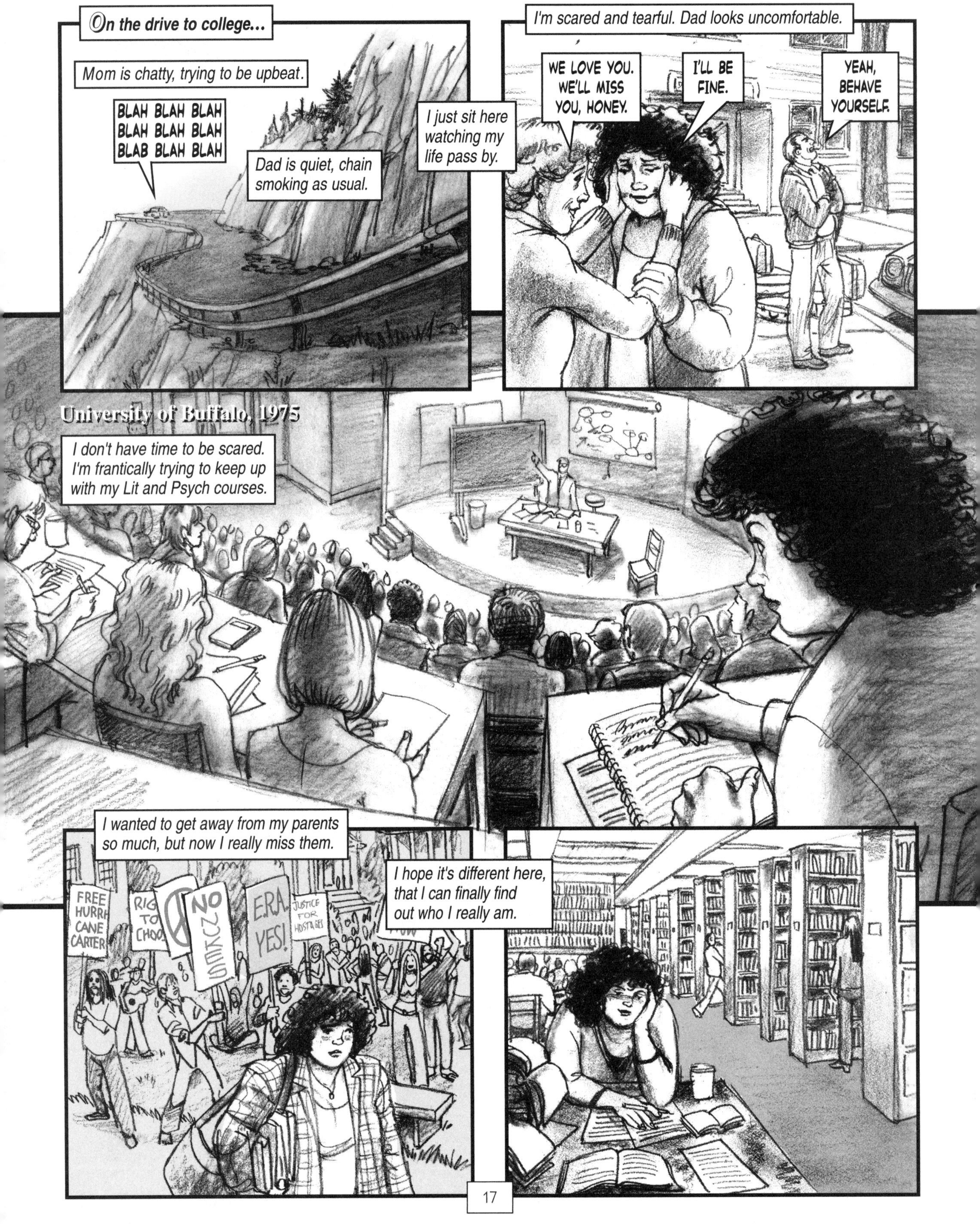
On the drive to college...
Mom is chatty, trying to be upbeat.
BLAH BLAH BLAH BLAH BLAH BLAH BLAB BLAH BLAH
Dad is quiet, chain smoking as usual.
I just sit here watching my life pass by.
I'm scared and tearful. Dad looks uncomfortable.
WE LOVE YOU. WE'LL MISS YOU, HONEY.
I'LL BE FINE.
YEAH, BEHAVE YOURSELF.
University of Buffalo, 1975
I don't have time to be scared. I'm frantically trying to keep up with my Lit and Psych courses.
I wanted to get away from my parents so much, but now I really miss them.
FREE HURRICANE CARTER
NO NUKES
E.R.A. YES!
JUSTICE FOR HOSTAGES
I hope it's different here, that I can finally find out who I really am.

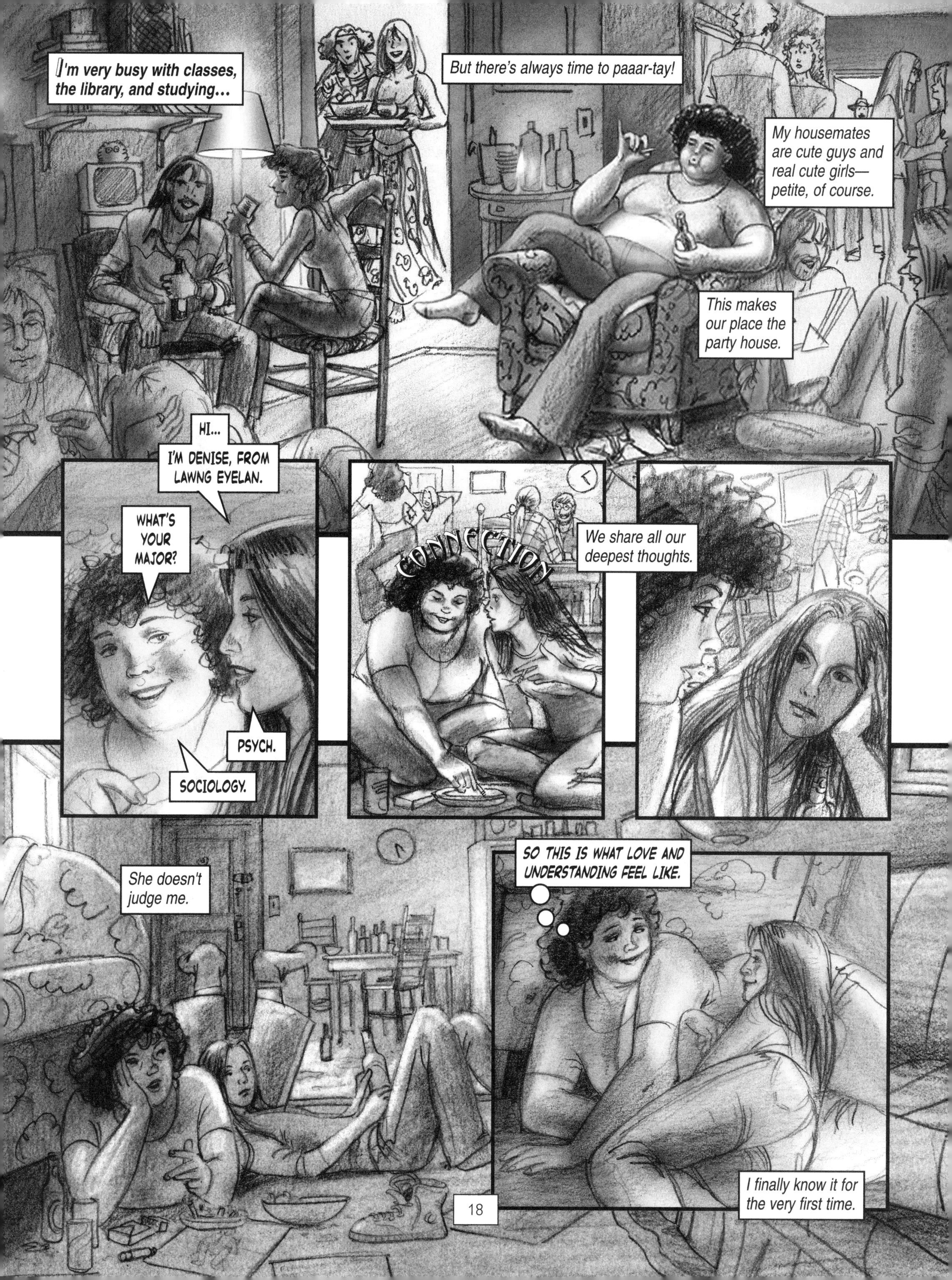
I'm very busy with classes, the library, and studying…
But there's always time to paaar-tay!
My housemates are cute guys and real cute girls—petite, of course.
This makes our place the party house.
HI…
I'M DENISE, FROM LAWNG EYELAN.
WHAT'S YOUR MAJOR?
PSYCH.
SOCIOLOGY.
CONNECTION
We share all our deepest thoughts.
She doesn't judge me.
SO THIS IS WHAT LOVE AND UNDERSTANDING FEEL LIKE.
I finally know it for the very first time.

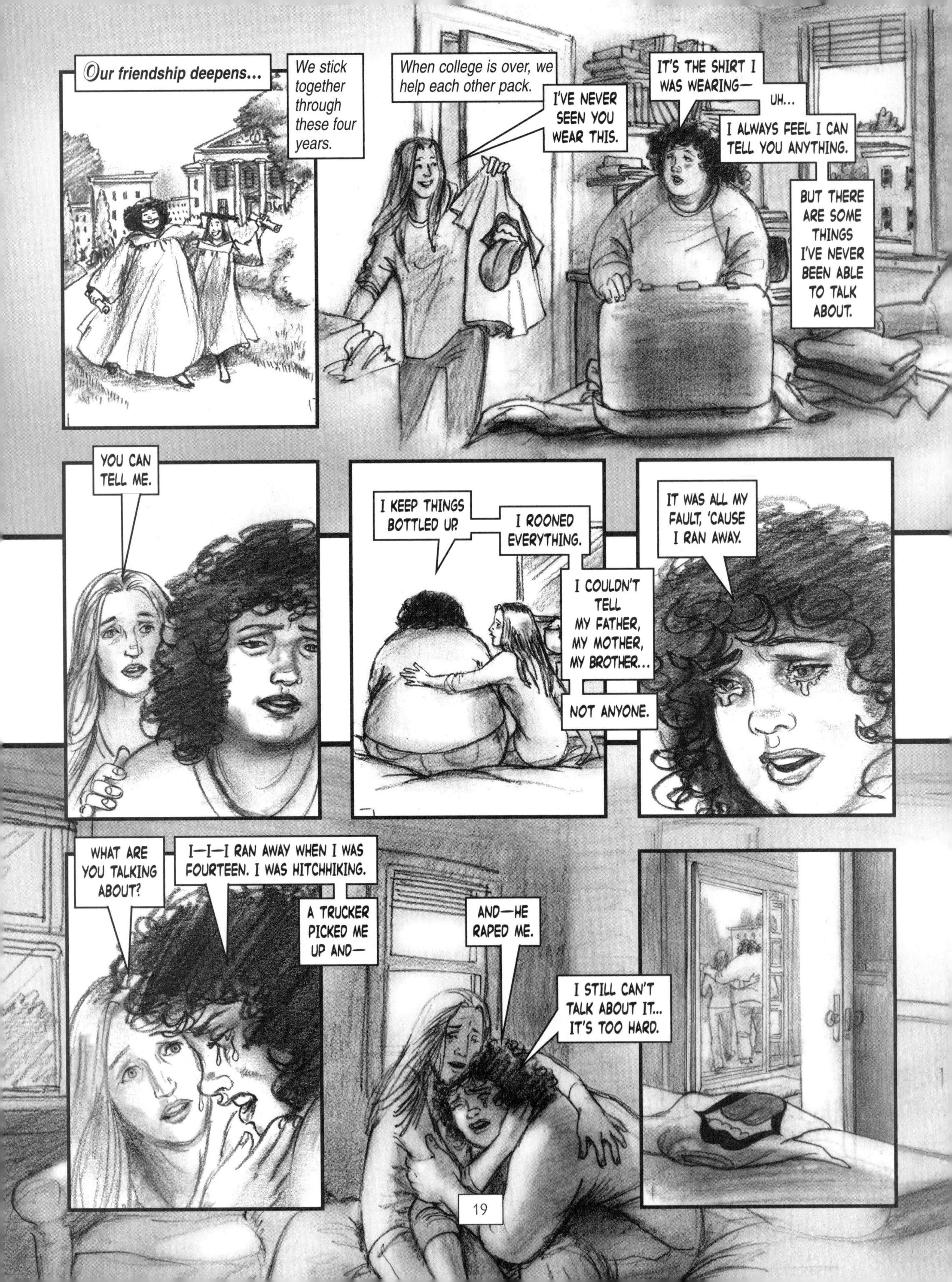
Our friendship deepens...
We stick together through these four years.
When college is over, we help each other pack.
I'VE NEVER SEEN YOU WEAR THIS.
IT'S THE SHIRT I WAS WEARING—
UH...
I ALWAYS FEEL I CAN TELL YOU ANYTHING.
BUT THERE ARE SOME THINGS I'VE NEVER BEEN ABLE TO TALK ABOUT.
YOU CAN TELL ME.
I KEEP THINGS BOTTLED UP.
I ROONED EVERYTHING.
I COULDN'T TELL MY FATHER, MY MOTHER, MY BROTHER...
NOT ANYONE.
IT WAS ALL MY FAULT, 'CAUSE I RAN AWAY.
WHAT ARE YOU TALKING ABOUT?
I—I—I RAN AWAY WHEN I WAS FOURTEEN. I WAS HITCHHIKING.
A TRUCKER PICKED ME UP AND—
AND—HE RAPED ME.
I STILL CAN'T TALK ABOUT IT... IT'S TOO HARD.

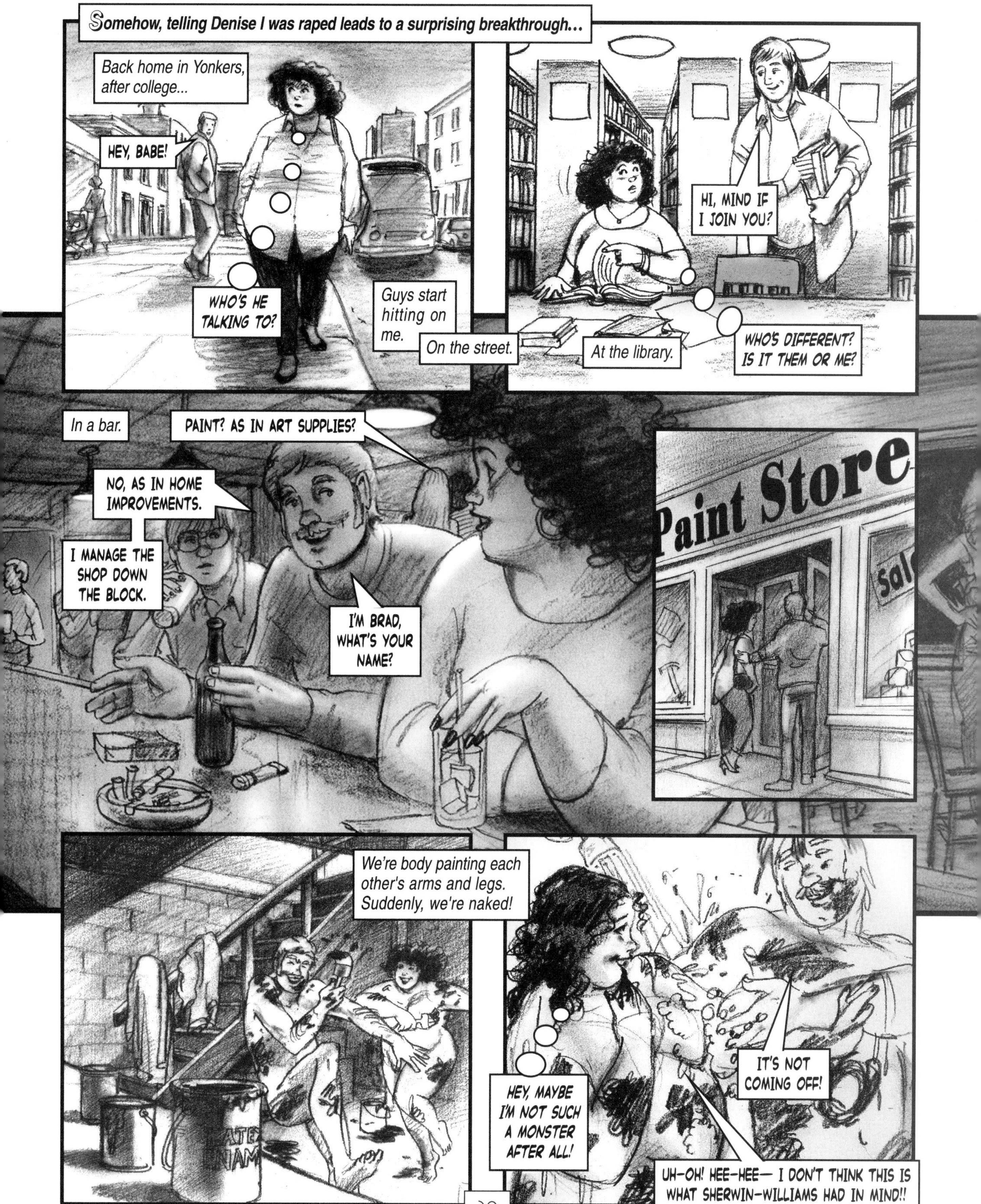
Somehow, telling Denise I was raped leads to a surprising breakthrough...
Back home in Yonkers, after college...
HEY, BABE!
WHO'S HE TALKING TO?
Guys start hitting on me.
On the street.
HI, MIND IF I JOIN YOU?
At the library.
WHO'S DIFFERENT? IS IT THEM OR ME?
In a bar.
PAINT? AS IN ART SUPPLIES?
NO, AS IN HOME IMPROVEMENTS.
I MANAGE THE SHOP DOWN THE BLOCK.
I'M BRAD, WHAT'S YOUR NAME?
Paint Store
We're body painting each other's arms and legs. Suddenly, we're naked!
HEY, MAYBE I'M NOT SUCH A MONSTER AFTER ALL!
IT'S NOT COMING OFF!
UH-OH! HEE-HEE— I DON'T THINK THIS IS WHAT SHERWIN-WILLIAMS HAD IN MIND!!

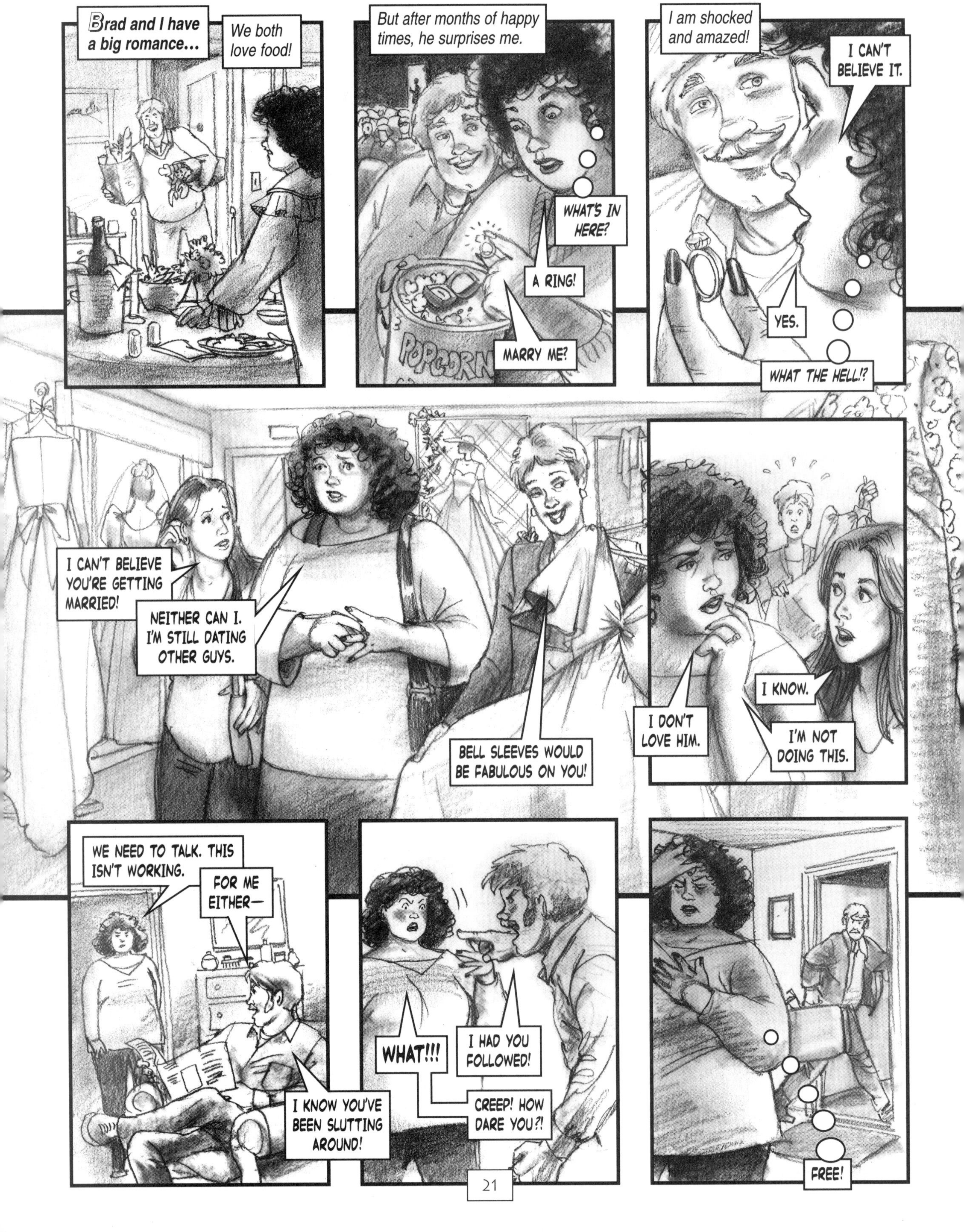
Brad and I have a big romance…
We both love food!
But after months of happy times, he surprises me.
WHAT'S IN HERE?
A RING!
MARRY ME?
I am shocked and amazed!
I CAN'T BELIEVE IT.
YES.
WHAT THE HELL!?
I CAN'T BELIEVE YOU'RE GETTING MARRIED!
NEITHER CAN I. I'M STILL DATING OTHER GUYS.
BELL SLEEVES WOULD BE FABULOUS ON YOU!
I DON'T LOVE HIM.
I KNOW.
I'M NOT DOING THIS.
WE NEED TO TALK. THIS ISN'T WORKING.
FOR ME EITHER—
I KNOW YOU'VE BEEN SLUTTING AROUND!
WHAT!!!
I HAD YOU FOLLOWED!
CREEP! HOW DARE YOU?!
FREE!

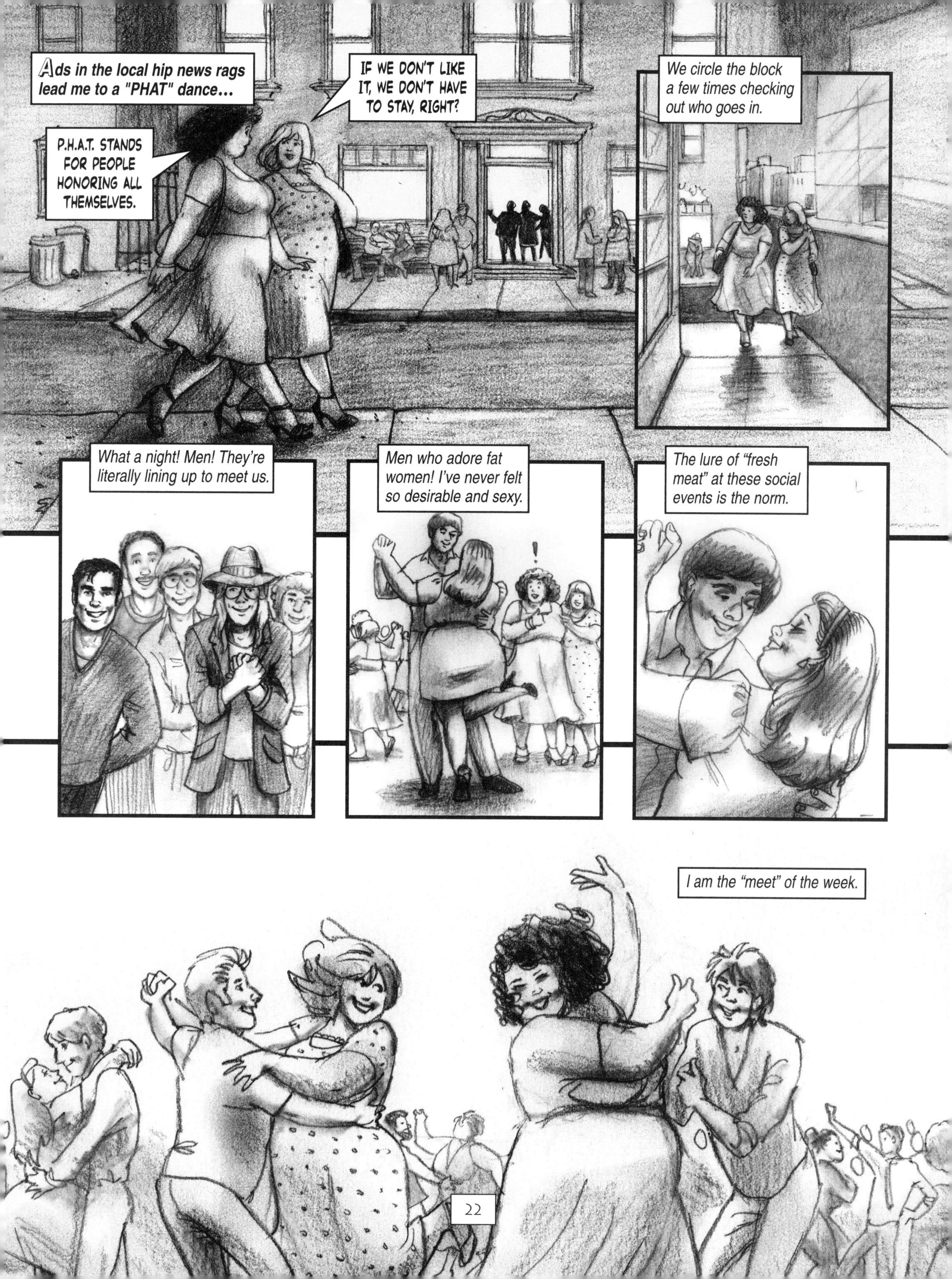
Ads in the local hip news rags lead me to a "PHAT" dance…
P.H.A.T. STANDS FOR PEOPLE HONORING ALL THEMSELVES.
IF WE DON'T LIKE IT, WE DON'T HAVE TO STAY, RIGHT?
We circle the block a few times checking out who goes in.
What a night! Men! They're literally lining up to meet us.
Men who adore fat women! I've never felt so desirable and sexy.
!
The lure of "fresh meat" at these social events is the norm.
I am the "meet" of the week.

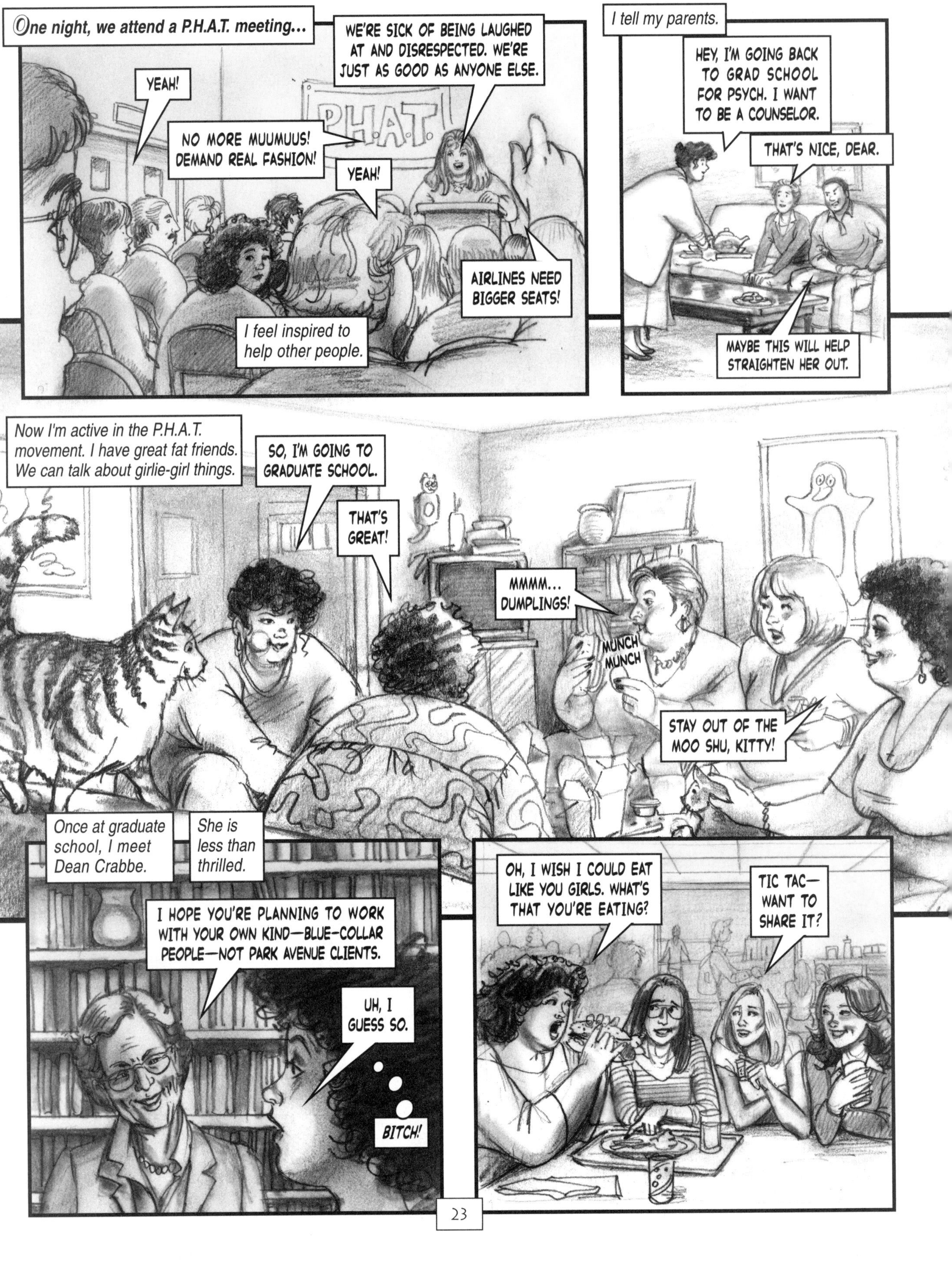

One night, we attend a P.H.A.T. meeting…
WE'RE SICK OF BEING LAUGHED AT AND DISRESPECTED. WE'RE JUST AS GOOD AS ANYONE ELSE.
YEAH!
P.H.A.T.
NO MORE MUUMUUS! DEMAND REAL FASHION!
YEAH!
AIRLINES NEED BIGGER SEATS!
I feel inspired to help other people.
I tell my parents.
HEY, I'M GOING BACK TO GRAD SCHOOL FOR PSYCH. I WANT TO BE A COUNSELOR.
THAT'S NICE, DEAR.
MAYBE THIS WILL HELP STRAIGHTEN HER OUT.
Now I'm active in the P.H.A.T. movement. I have great fat friends. We can talk about girlie-girl things.
SO, I'M GOING TO GRADUATE SCHOOL.
THAT'S GREAT!
MMMM… DUMPLINGS!
MUNCH MUNCH
STAY OUT OF THE MOO SHU, KITTY!
Once at graduate school, I meet Dean Crabbe.
She is less than thrilled.
I HOPE YOU'RE PLANNING TO WORK WITH YOUR OWN KIND—BLUE-COLLAR PEOPLE—NOT PARK AVENUE CLIENTS.
UH, I GUESS SO.
BITCH!
OH, I WISH I COULD EAT LIKE YOU GIRLS. WHAT'S THAT YOU'RE EATING?
TIC TAC—WANT TO SHARE IT?

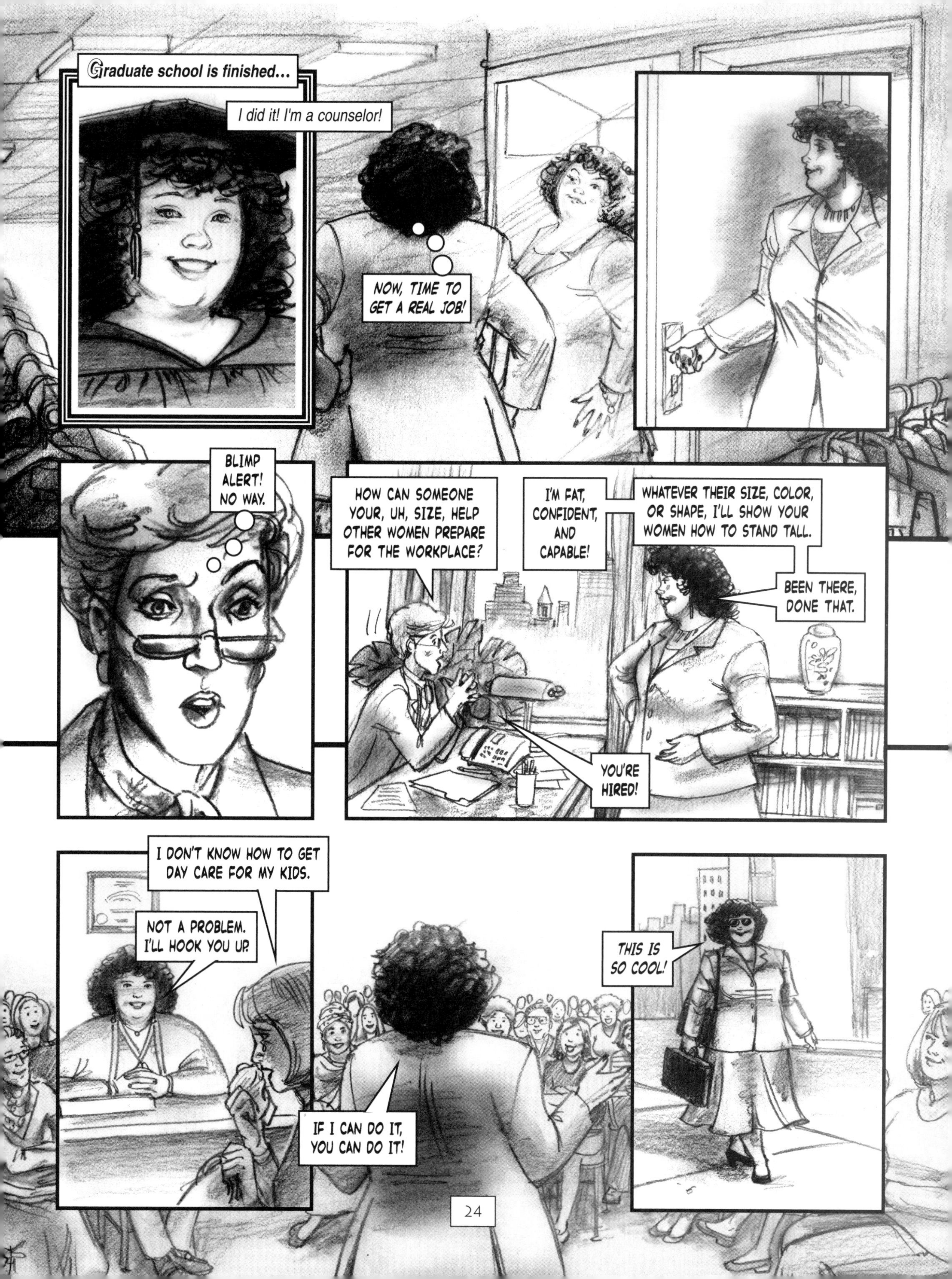
Graduate school is finished...
I did it! I'm a counselor!
NOW, TIME TO GET A REAL JOB!
BLIMP ALERT! NO WAY.
HOW CAN SOMEONE YOUR, UH, SIZE, HELP OTHER WOMEN PREPARE FOR THE WORKPLACE?
I'M FAT, CONFIDENT, AND CAPABLE!
WHATEVER THEIR SIZE, COLOR, OR SHAPE, I'LL SHOW YOUR WOMEN HOW TO STAND TALL.
BEEN THERE, DONE THAT.
YOU'RE HIRED!
I DON'T KNOW HOW TO GET DAY CARE FOR MY KIDS.
NOT A PROBLEM. I'LL HOOK YOU UP.
IF I CAN DO IT, YOU CAN DO IT!
THIS IS SO COOL!

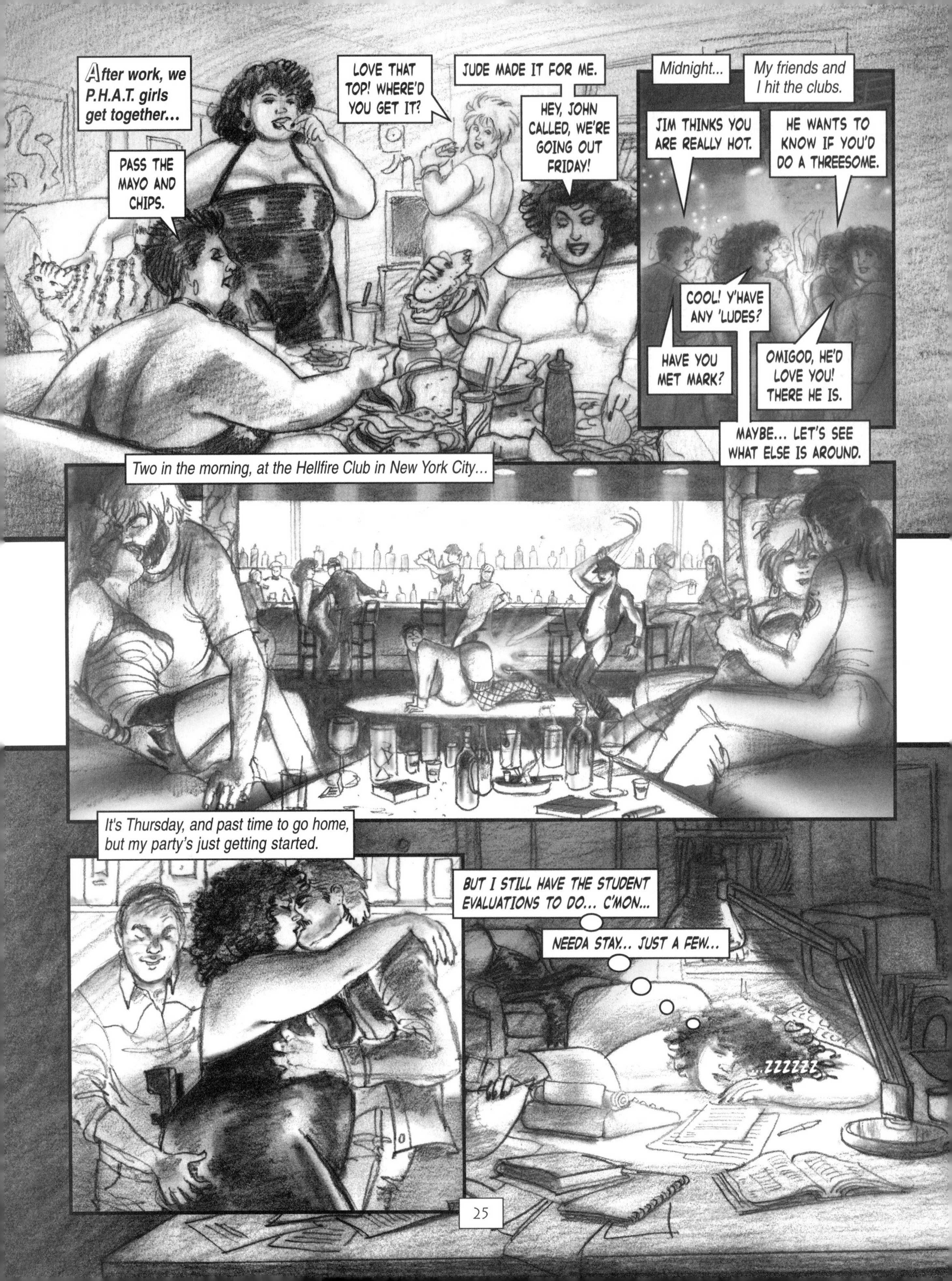
After work, we P.H.A.T. girls get together…
PASS THE MAYO AND CHIPS.
LOVE THAT TOP! WHERE'D YOU GET IT?
JUDE MADE IT FOR ME.
HEY, JOHN CALLED, WE'RE GOING OUT FRIDAY!
Midnight…
My friends and I hit the clubs.
JIM THINKS YOU ARE REALLY HOT.
HE WANTS TO KNOW IF YOU'D DO A THREESOME.
COOL! Y'HAVE ANY 'LUDES?
HAVE YOU MET MARK?
OMIGOD, HE'D LOVE YOU! THERE HE IS.
MAYBE… LET'S SEE WHAT ELSE IS AROUND.
Two in the morning, at the Hellfire Club in New York City…
It's Thursday, and past time to go home, but my party's just getting started.
BUT I STILL HAVE THE STUDENT EVALUATIONS TO DO… C'MON…
NEEDA STAY… JUST A FEW…
…ZZZZZZ

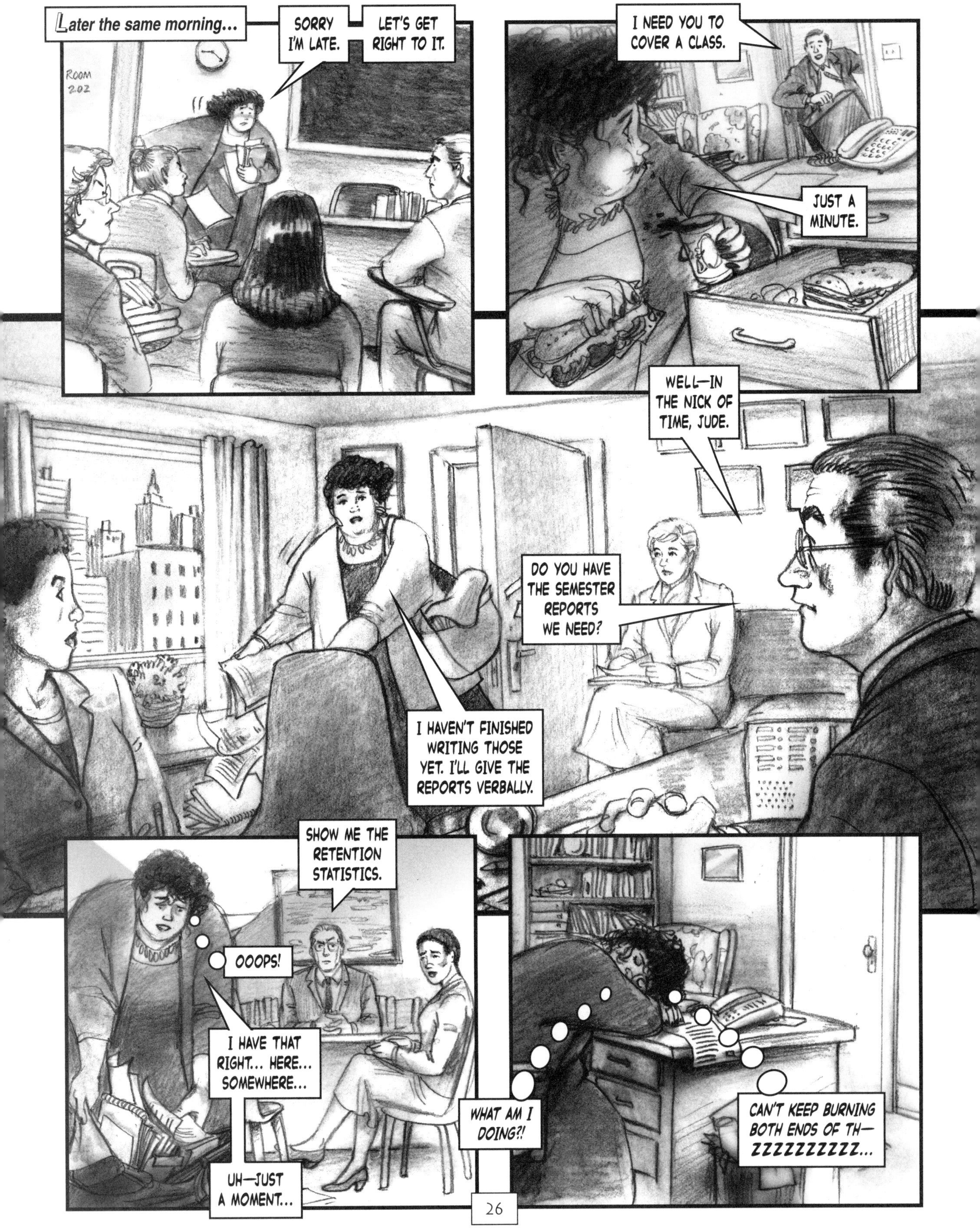
Later the same morning...
ROOM 202
SORRY I'M LATE.
LET'S GET RIGHT TO IT.
I NEED YOU TO COVER A CLASS.
JUST A MINUTE.
WELL—IN THE NICK OF TIME, JUDE.
DO YOU HAVE THE SEMESTER REPORTS WE NEED?
I HAVEN'T FINISHED WRITING THOSE YET. I'LL GIVE THE REPORTS VERBALLY.
SHOW ME THE RETENTION STATISTICS.
OOOPS!
I HAVE THAT RIGHT... HERE... SOMEWHERE...
UH—JUST A MOMENT...
WHAT AM I DOING?!
CAN'T KEEP BURNING BOTH ENDS OF TH—ZZZZZZZZZZ...

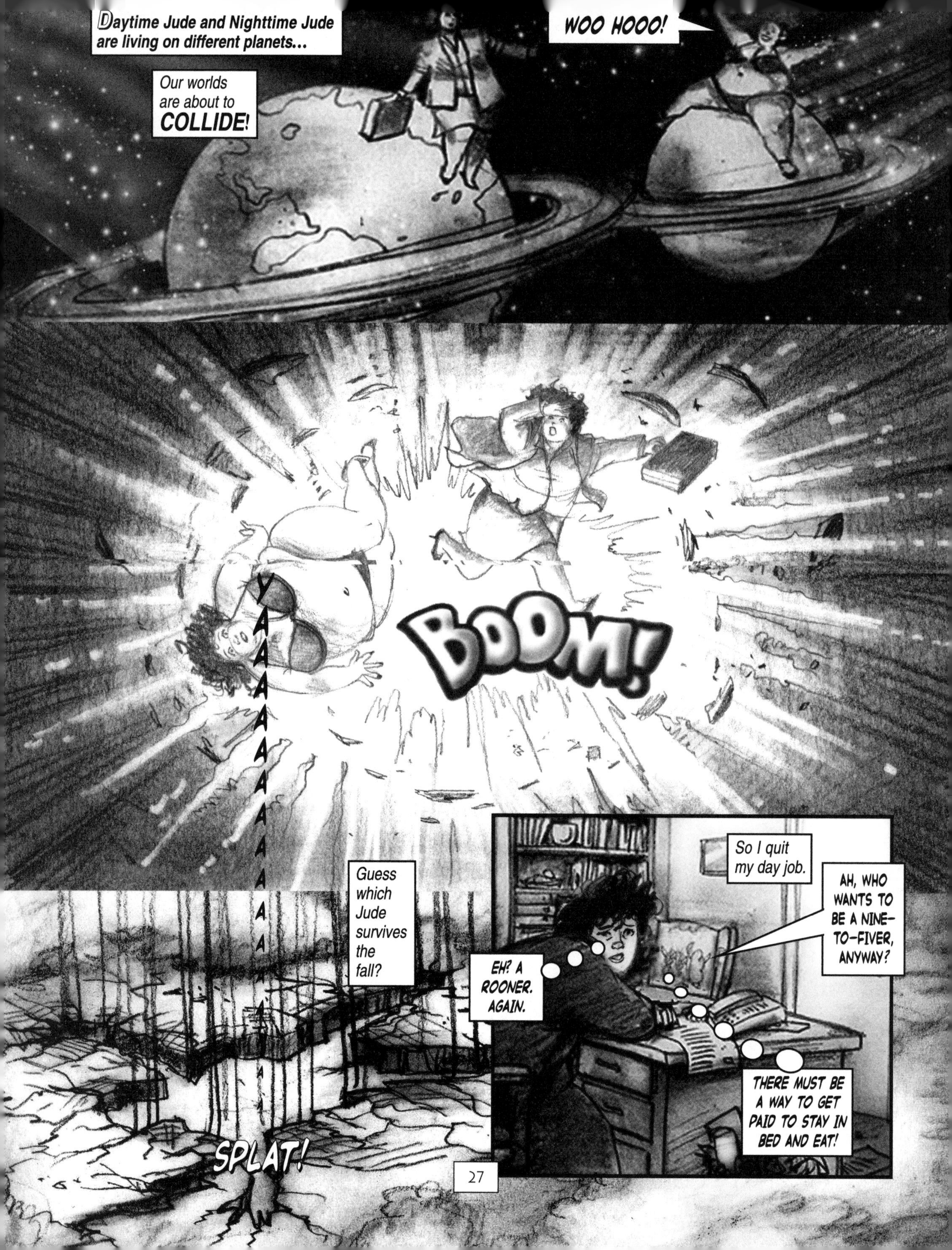
Daytime Jude and Nighttime Jude are living on different planets...
WOO HOOO!
Our worlds are about to COLLIDE!
BOOM!
Guess which Jude survives the fall?
SPLAT!
So I quit my day job.
AH, WHO WANTS TO BE A NINE-TO-FIVER, ANYWAY?
EH? A ROONER. AGAIN.
THERE MUST BE A WAY TO GET PAID TO STAY IN BED AND EAT!

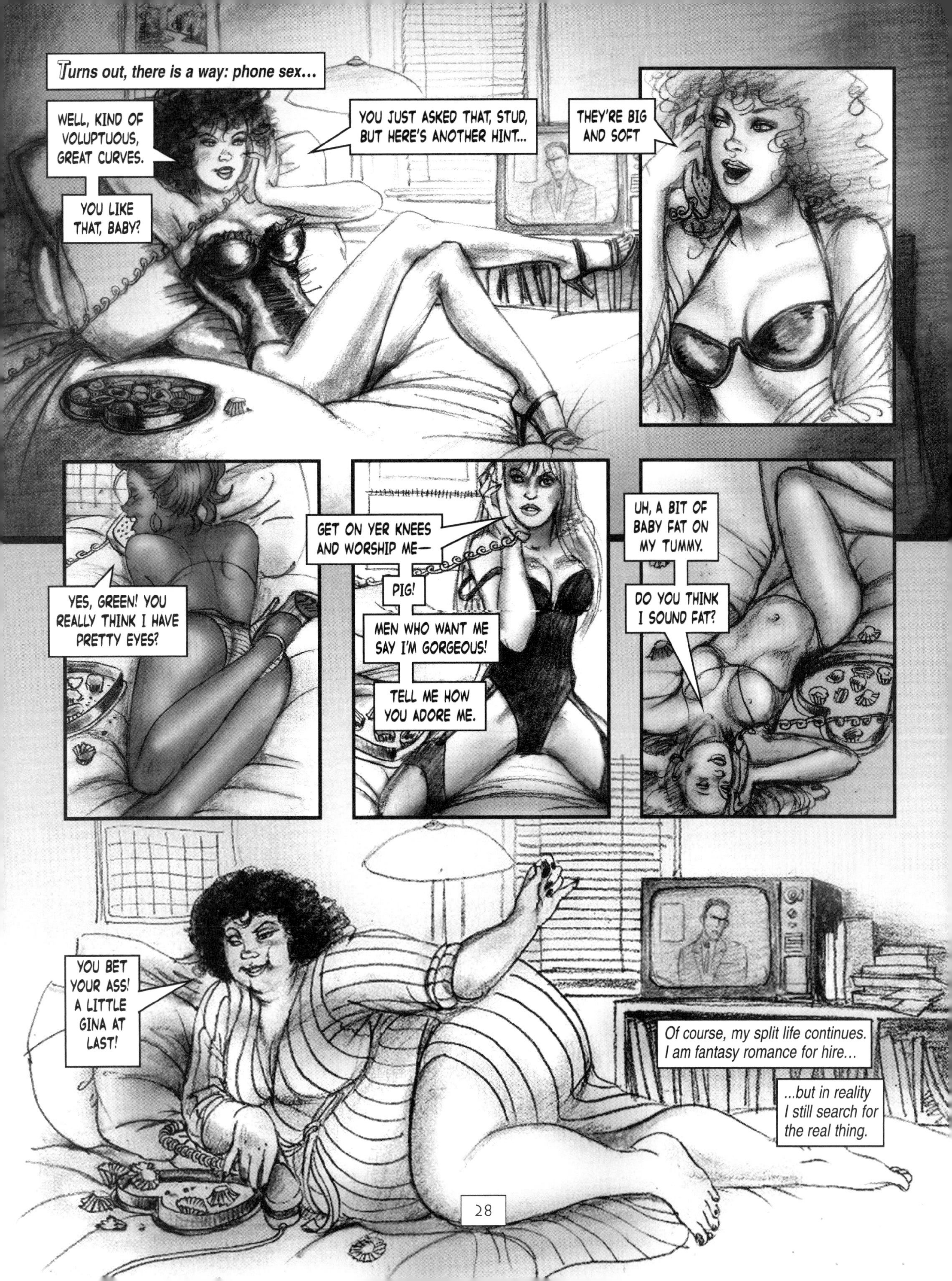
Turns out, there is a way: phone sex…
WELL, KIND OF VOLUPTUOUS, GREAT CURVES.
YOU LIKE THAT, BABY?
YOU JUST ASKED THAT, STUD, BUT HERE'S ANOTHER HINT...
THEY'RE BIG AND SOFT
YES, GREEN! YOU REALLY THINK I HAVE PRETTY EYES?
GET ON YER KNEES AND WORSHIP ME—
PIG!
MEN WHO WANT ME SAY I'M GORGEOUS!
TELL ME HOW YOU ADORE ME.
UH, A BIT OF BABY FAT ON MY TUMMY.
DO YOU THINK I SOUND FAT?
YOU BET YOUR ASS! A LITTLE GINA AT LAST!
Of course, my split life continues. I am fantasy romance for hire…
...but in reality I still search for the real thing.

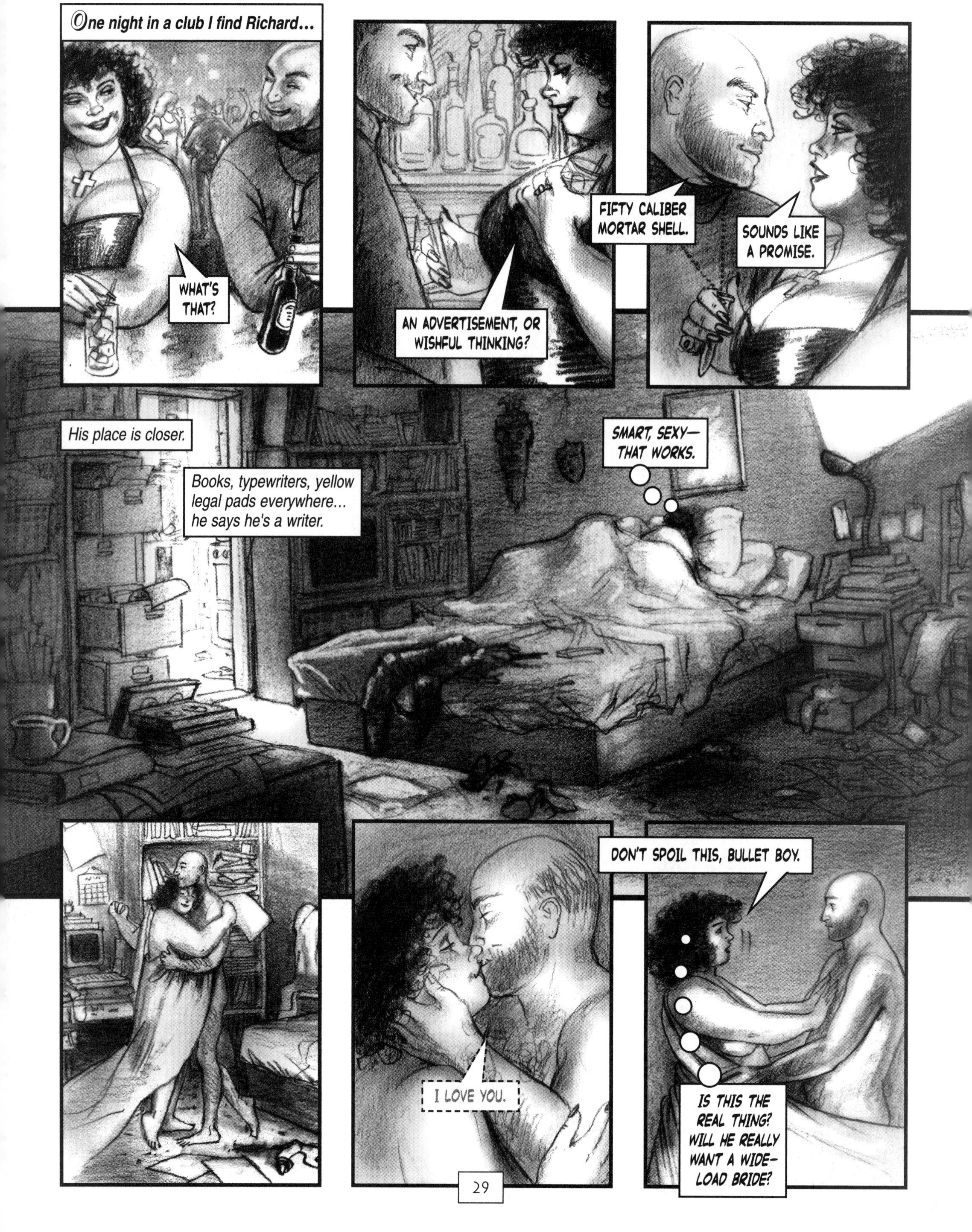
One night in a club I find Richard…
WHAT'S THAT?
AN ADVERTISEMENT, OR WISHFUL THINKING?
FIFTY CALIBER MORTAR SHELL.
SOUNDS LIKE A PROMISE.
His place is closer.
Books, typewriters, yellow legal pads everywhere… he says he's a writer.
SMART, SEXY— THAT WORKS.
I LOVE YOU.
DON'T SPOIL THIS, BULLET BOY.
IS THIS THE REAL THING? WILL HE REALLY WANT A WIDE-LOAD BRIDE?

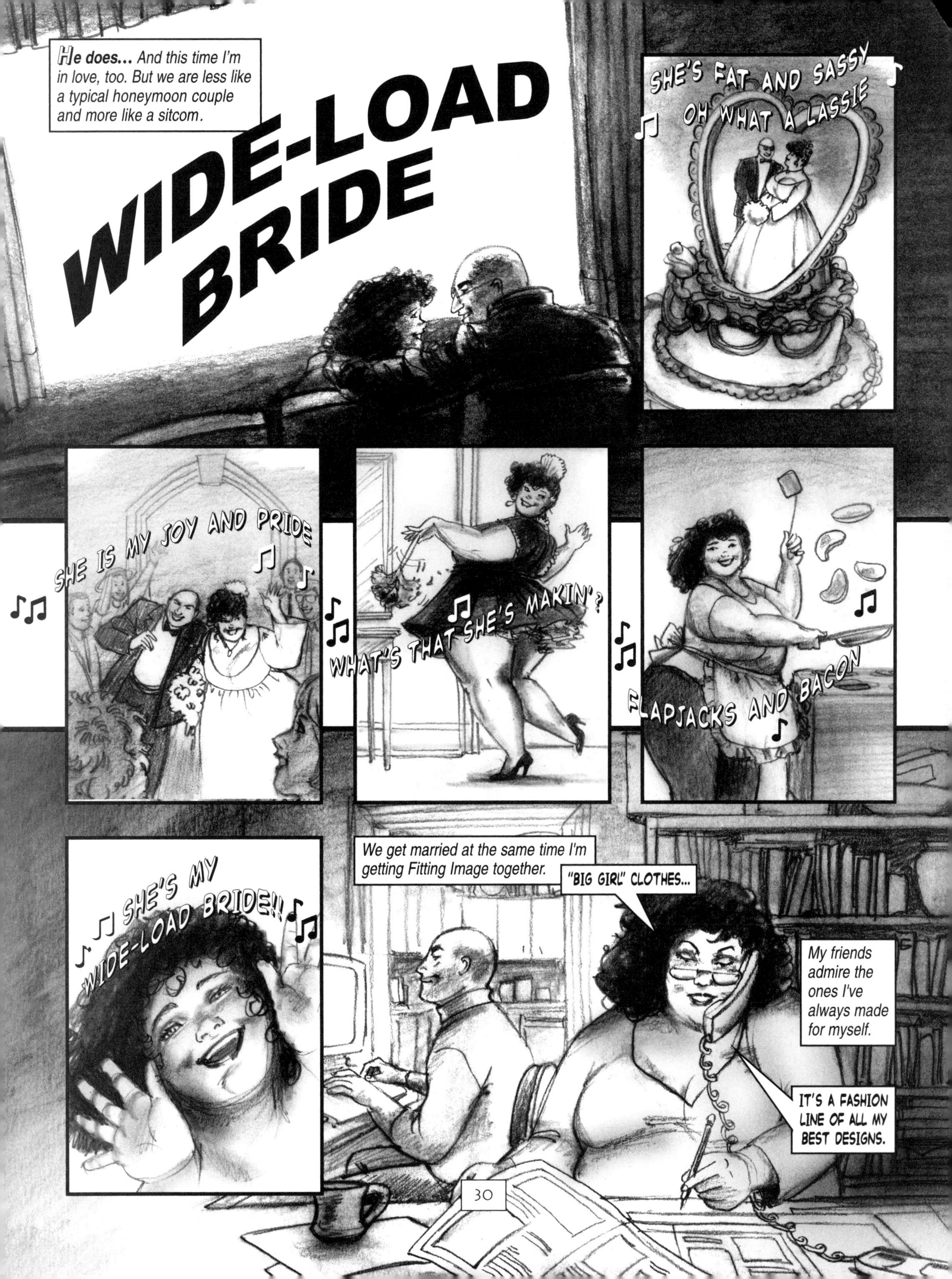

He does... And this time I'm in love, too. But we are less like a typical honeymoon couple and more like a sitcom.
WIDE-LOAD BRIDE
SHE'S FAT AND SASSY
OH WHAT A LASSIE
SHE IS MY JOY AND PRIDE
WHAT'S THAT SHE'S MAKIN'?
FLAPJACKS AND BACON
SHE'S MY WIDE-LOAD BRIDE!!
We get married at the same time I'm getting Fitting Image together.
"BIG GIRL" CLOTHES...
My friends admire the ones I've always made for myself.
IT'S A FASHION LINE OF ALL MY BEST DESIGNS.

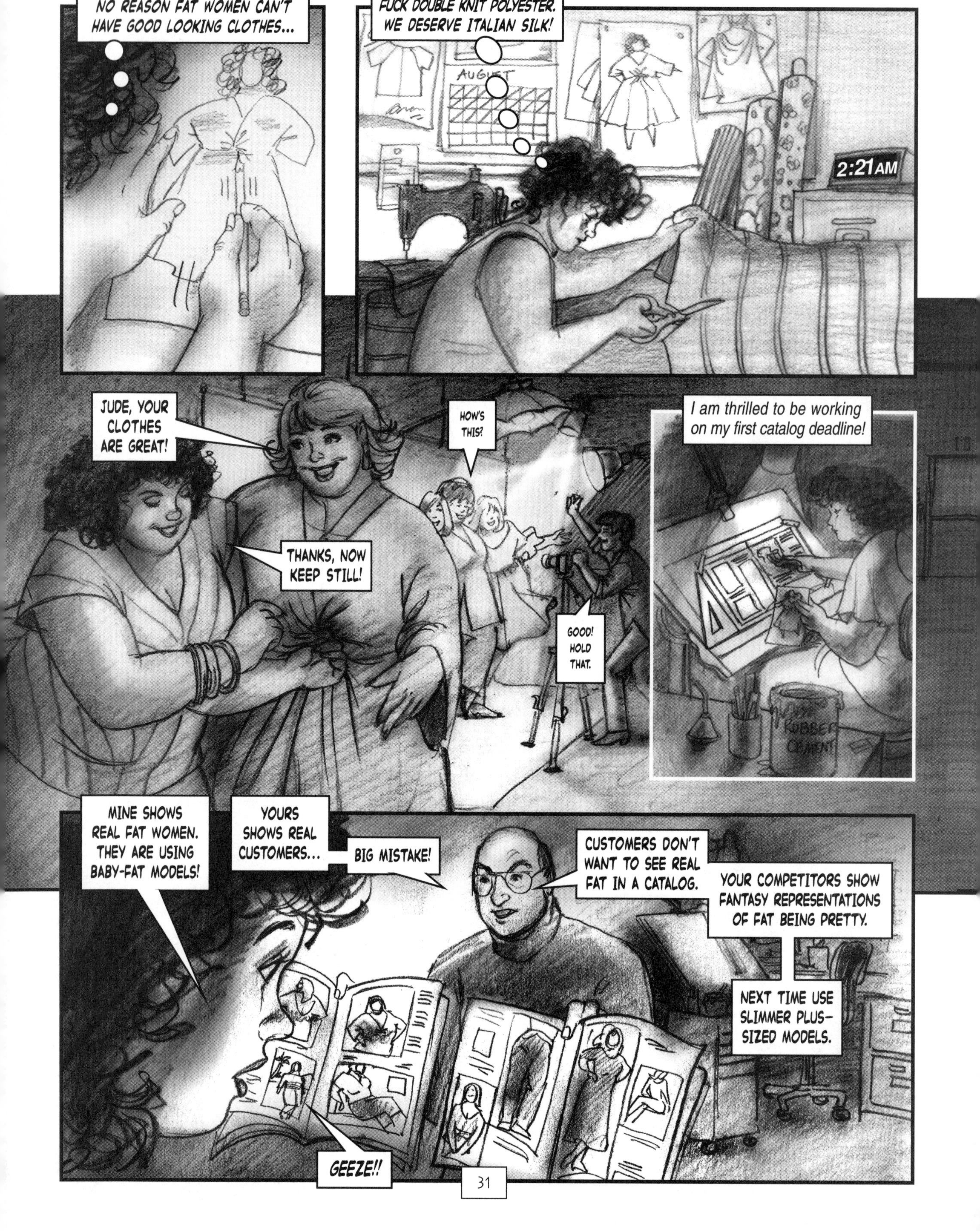
NO REASON FAT WOMEN CAN'T HAVE GOOD LOOKING CLOTHES...
FUCK DOUBLE KNIT POLYESTER. WE DESERVE ITALIAN SILK!
AUGUST
2:21AM
JUDE, YOUR CLOTHES ARE GREAT!
THANKS, NOW KEEP STILL!
HOW'S THIS?
GOOD! HOLD THAT.
I am thrilled to be working on my first catalog deadline!
RUBBER CEMENT
MINE SHOWS REAL FAT WOMEN. THEY ARE USING BABY-FAT MODELS!
YOURS SHOWS REAL CUSTOMERS...
BIG MISTAKE!
CUSTOMERS DON'T WANT TO SEE REAL FAT IN A CATALOG.
YOUR COMPETITORS SHOW FANTASY REPRESENTATIONS OF FAT BEING PRETTY.
NEXT TIME USE SLIMMER PLUS-SIZED MODELS.
GEEZE!!

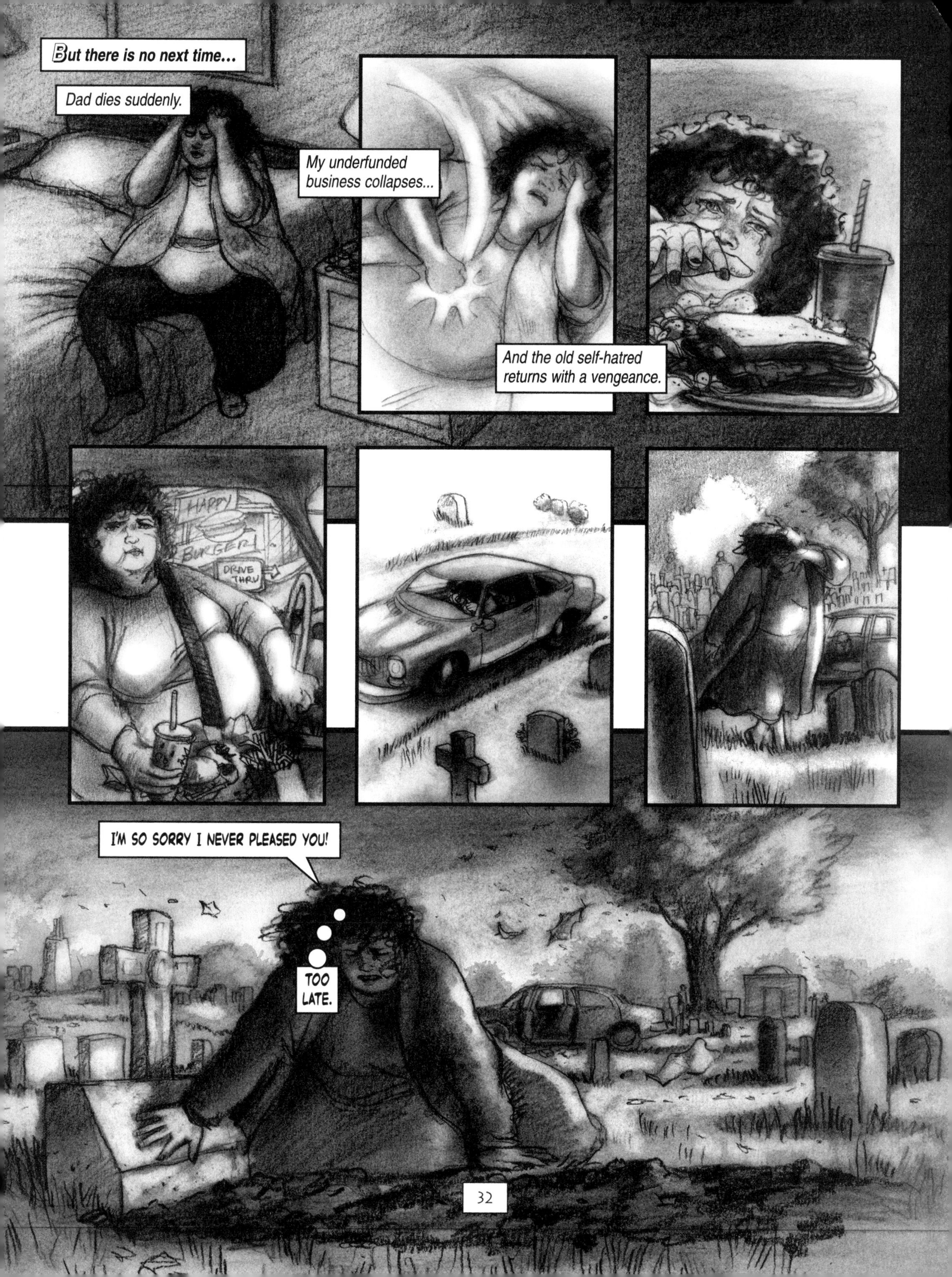
But there is no next time...
Dad dies suddenly.
My underfunded business collapses...
And the old self-hatred returns with a vengeance.
HAPPY BURGER
DRIVE THRU
I'M SO SORRY I NEVER PLEASED YOU!
TOO LATE.

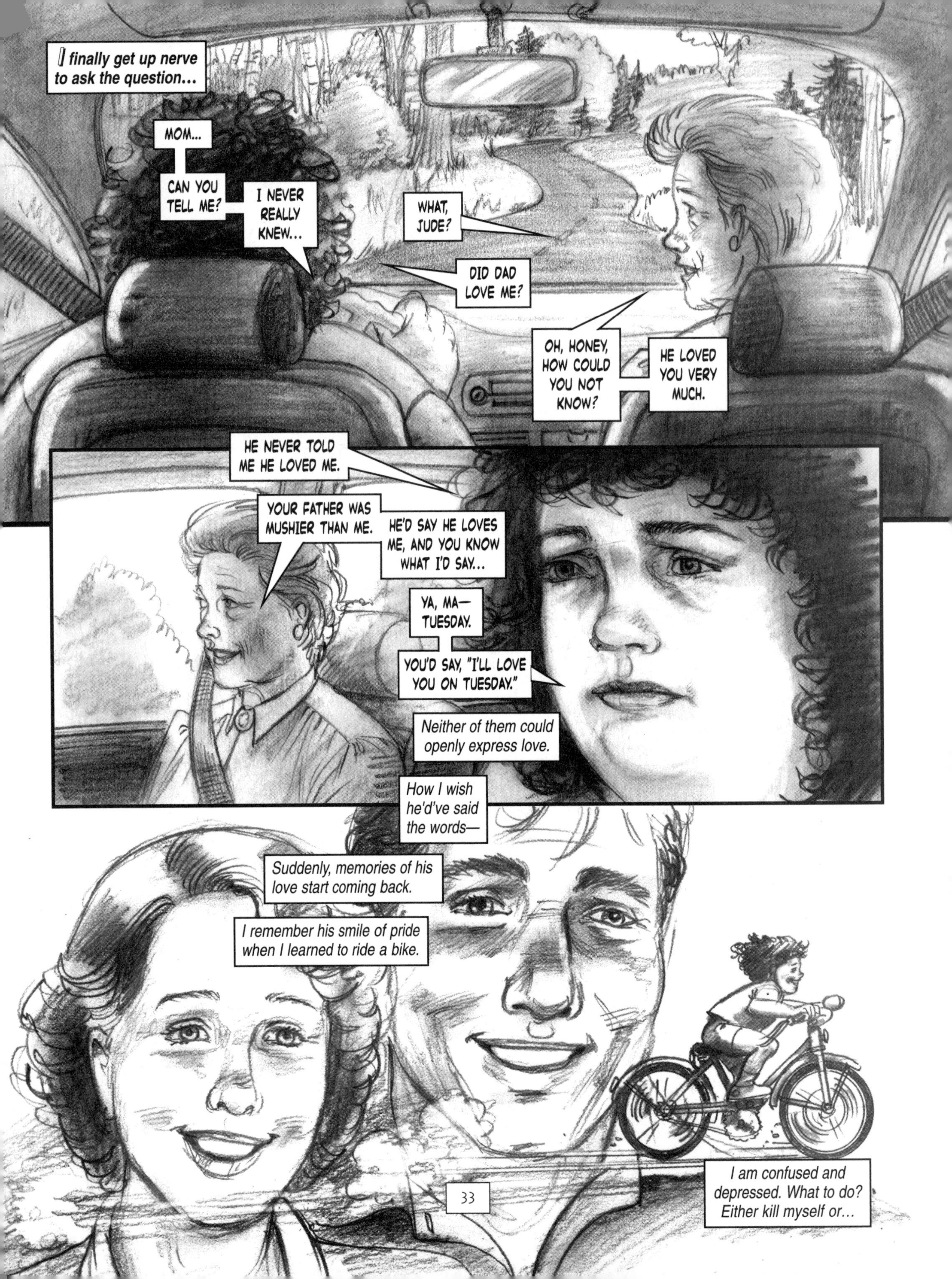
I finally get up nerve to ask the question...
MOM...
CAN YOU TELL ME?
I NEVER REALLY KNEW...
WHAT, JUDE?
DID DAD LOVE ME?
OH, HONEY, HOW COULD YOU NOT KNOW?
HE LOVED YOU VERY MUCH.
HE NEVER TOLD ME HE LOVED ME.
YOUR FATHER WAS MUSHIER THAN ME.
HE'D SAY HE LOVES ME, AND YOU KNOW WHAT I'D SAY...
YA, MA— TUESDAY.
YOU'D SAY, "I'LL LOVE YOU ON TUESDAY."
Neither of them could openly express love.
How I wish he'd've said the words—
Suddenly, memories of his love start coming back.
I remember his smile of pride when I learned to ride a bike.
I am confused and depressed. What to do? Either kill myself or...

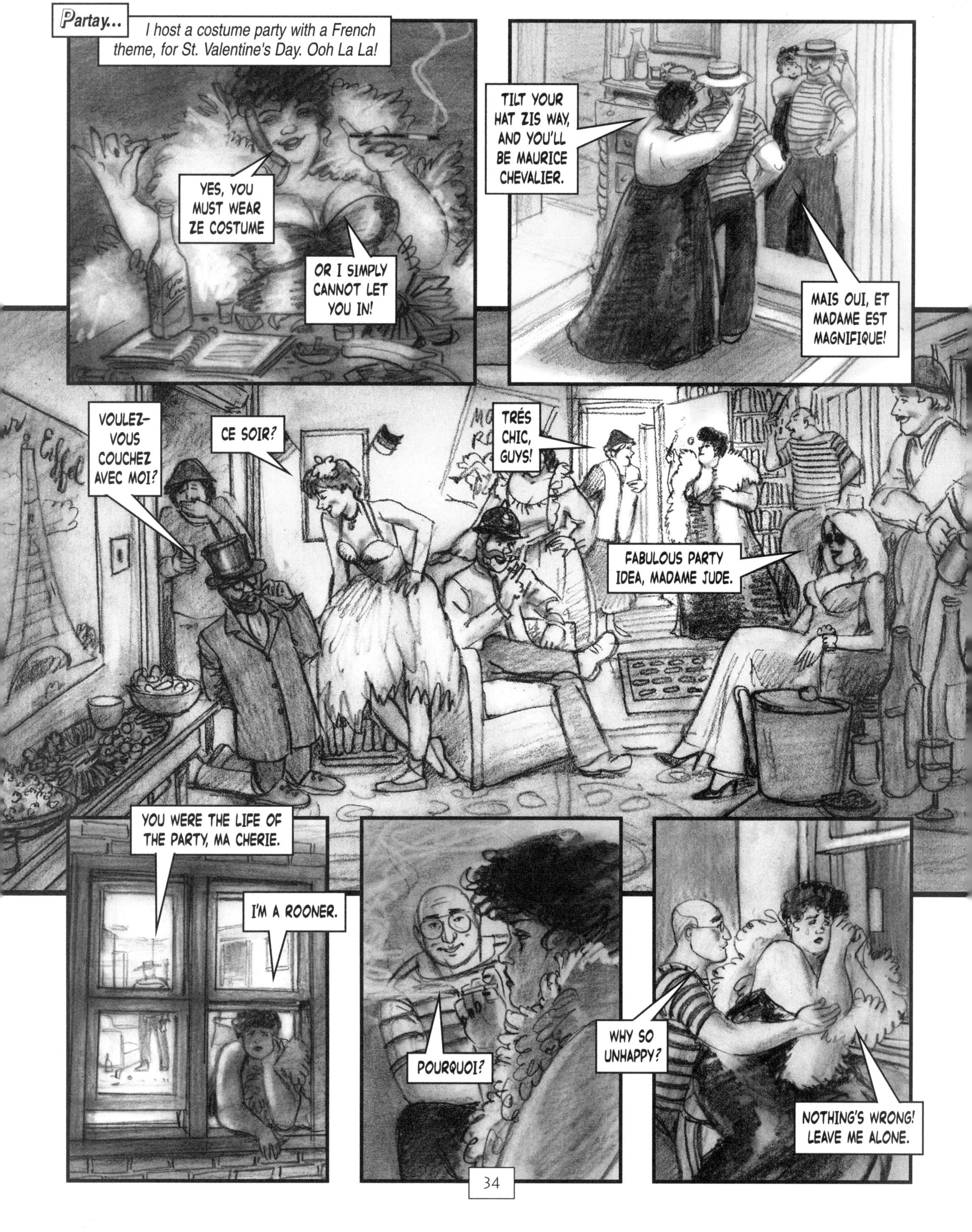
Partay...
I host a costume party with a French theme, for St. Valentine's Day. Ooh La La!
YES, YOU MUST WEAR ZE COSTUME
OR I SIMPLY CANNOT LET YOU IN!
TILT YOUR HAT ZIS WAY, AND YOU'LL BE MAURICE CHEVALIER.
MAIS OUI, ET MADAME EST MAGNIFIQUE!
VOULEZ-VOUS COUCHEZ AVEC MOI?
CE SOIR?
TRÉS CHIC, GUYS!
FABULOUS PARTY IDEA, MADAME JUDE.
YOU WERE THE LIFE OF THE PARTY, MA CHERIE.
I'M A ROONER.
POURQUOI?
WHY SO UNHAPPY?
NOTHING'S WRONG! LEAVE ME ALONE.

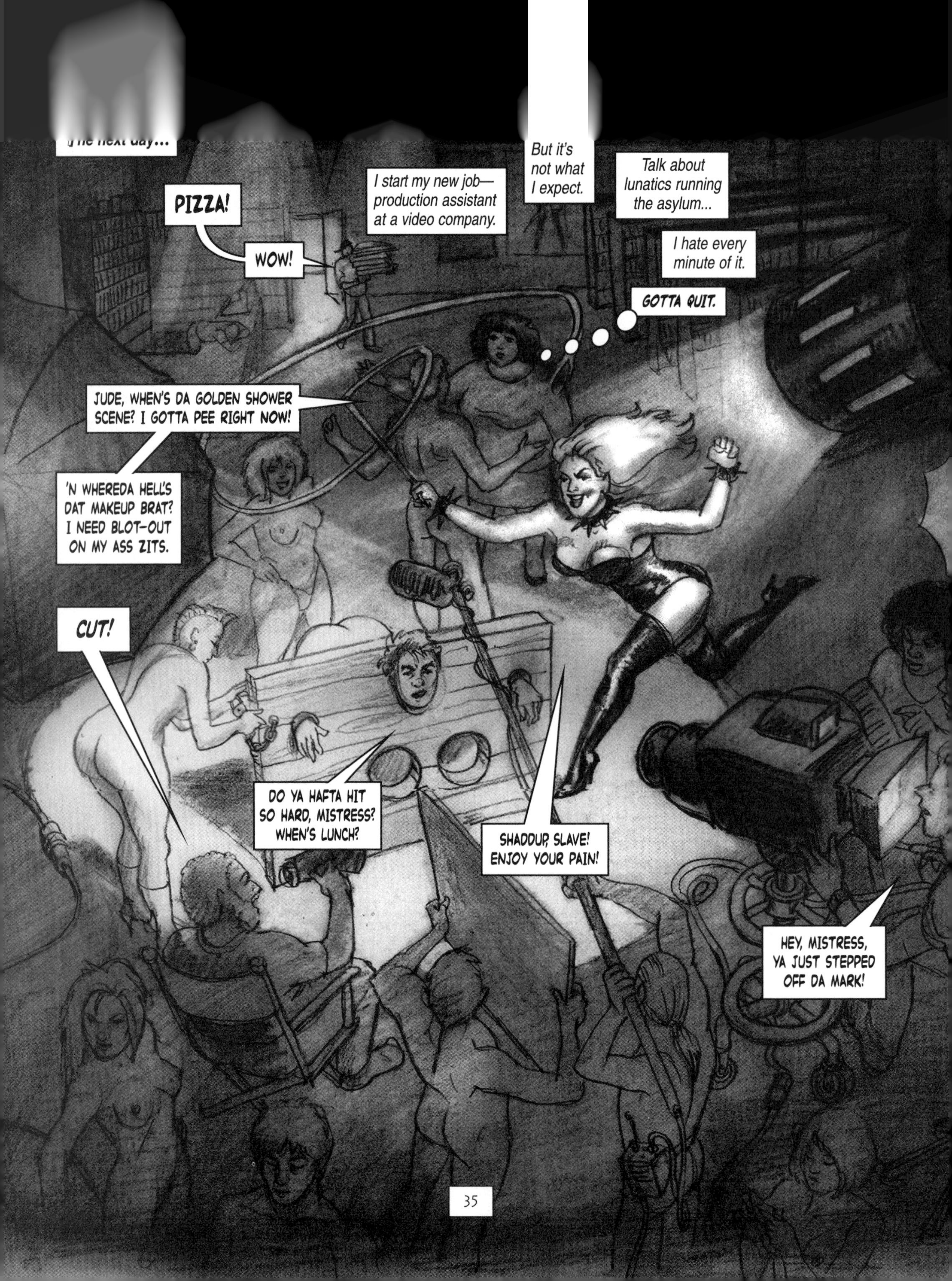
PIZZA!
WOW!
I start my new job— production assistant at a video company.
But it's not what I expect.
Talk about lunatics running the asylum...
I hate every minute of it.
GOTTA QUIT.
JUDE, WHEN'S DA GOLDEN SHOWER SCENE? I GOTTA PEE RIGHT NOW!
'N WHEREDA HELL'S DAT MAKEUP BRAT? I NEED BLOT-OUT ON MY ASS ZITS.
CUT!
DO YA HAFTA HIT SO HARD, MISTRESS? WHEN'S LUNCH?
SHADDUP, SLAVE! ENJOY YOUR PAIN!
HEY, MISTRESS, YA JUST STEPPED OFF DA MARK!

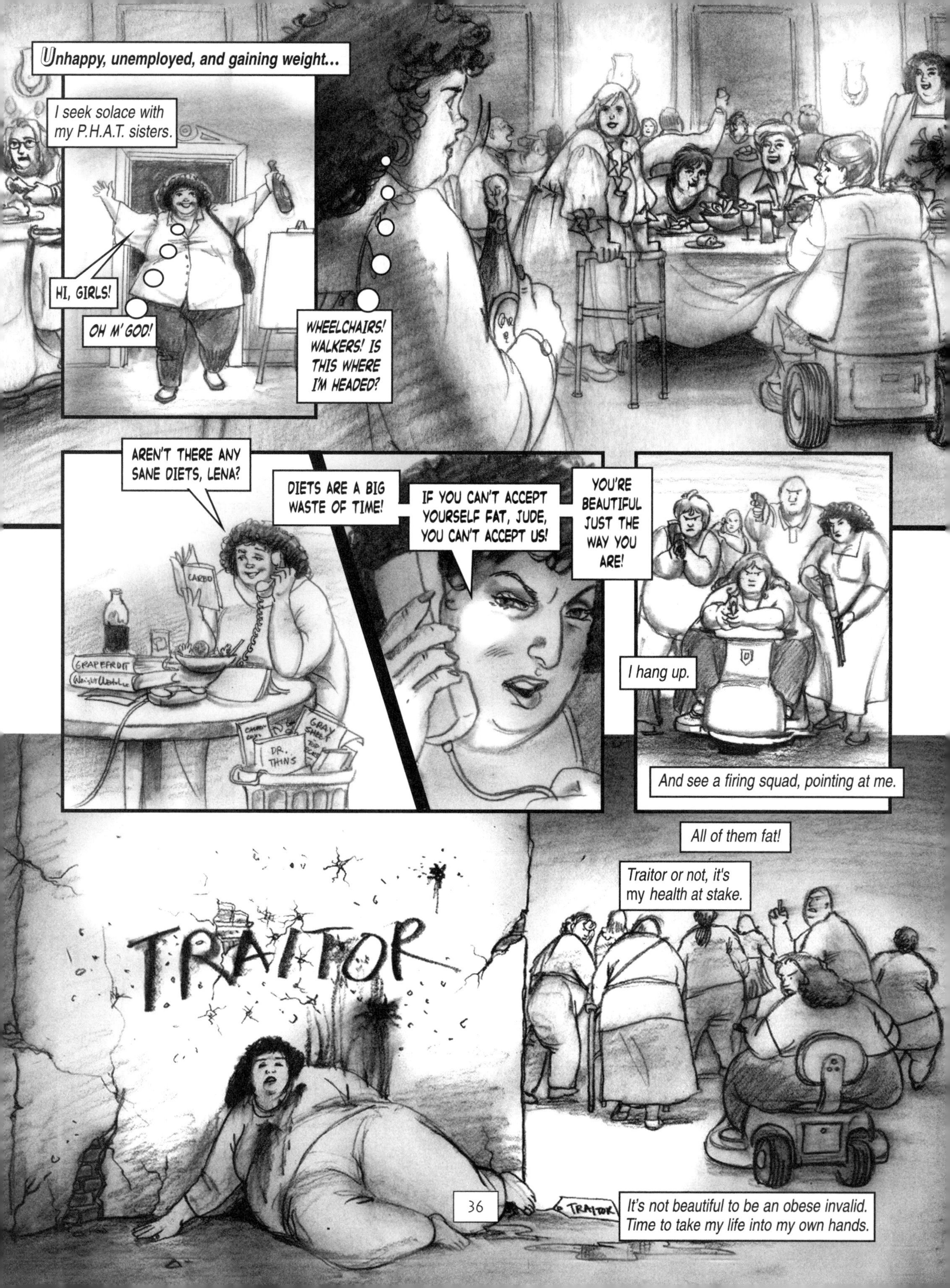
Unhappy, unemployed, and gaining weight…
I seek solace with my P.H.A.T. sisters.
HI, GIRLS!
OH M' GOD!
WHEELCHAIRS! WALKERS! IS THIS WHERE I'M HEADED?
AREN'T THERE ANY SANE DIETS, LENA?
CARBO
GRAPEFRUIT
DR.
GRAY SHEET
DIETS ARE A BIG WASTE OF TIME!
IF YOU CAN'T ACCEPT YOURSELF FAT, JUDE, YOU CAN'T ACCEPT US!
YOU'RE BEAUTIFUL JUST THE WAY YOU ARE!
I hang up.
And see a firing squad, pointing at me.
All of them fat!
Traitor or not, it's my health at stake.
TRAITOR
It's not beautiful to be an obese invalid. Time to take my life into my own hands.

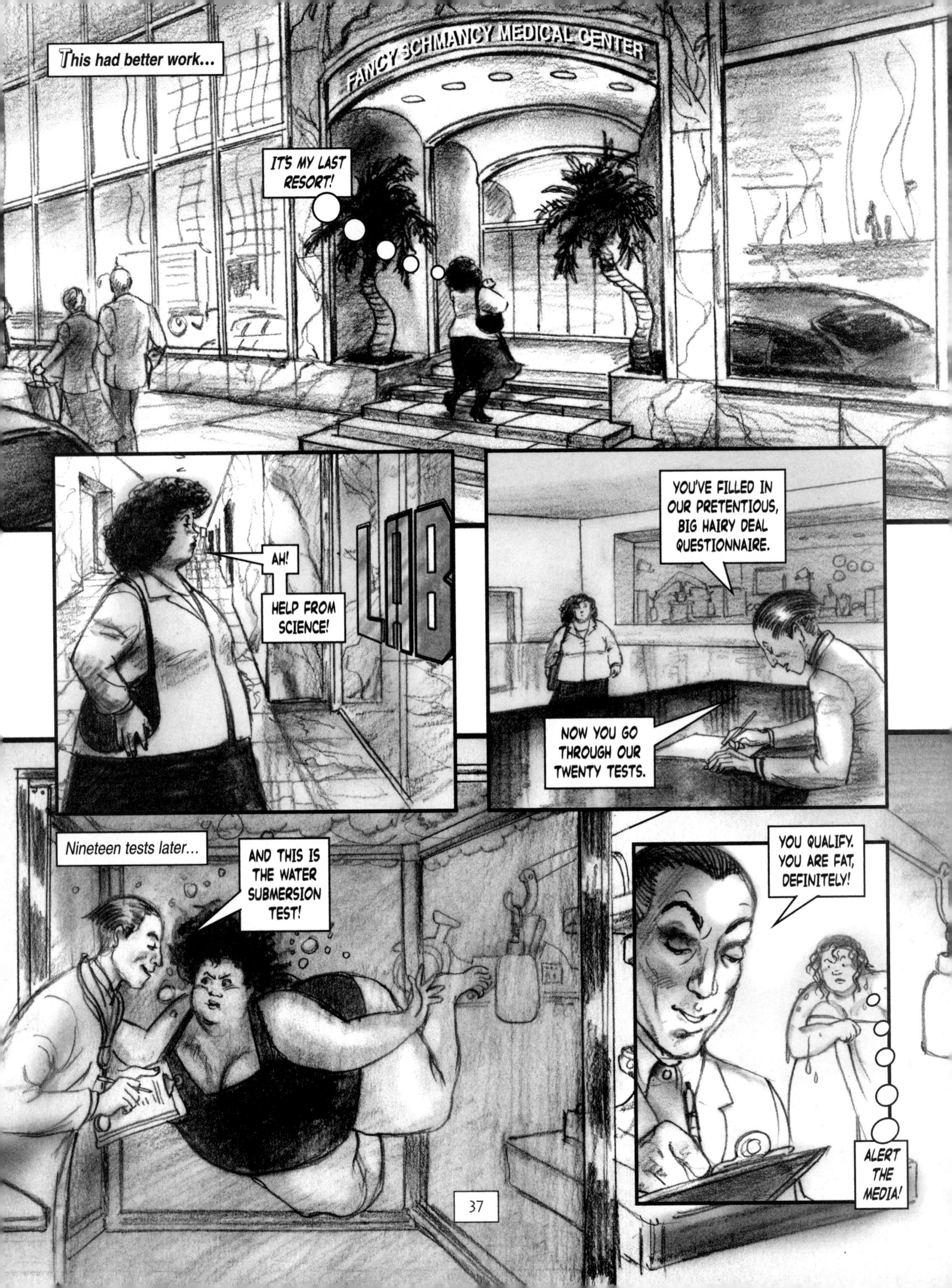
This had better work...
FANCY SCHMANCY MEDICAL CENTER
IT'S MY LAST RESORT!
AH!
HELP FROM SCIENCE!
LAB
YOU'VE FILLED IN OUR PRETENTIOUS, BIG HAIRY DEAL QUESTIONNAIRE.
NOW YOU GO THROUGH OUR TWENTY TESTS.
Nineteen tests later...
AND THIS IS THE WATER SUBMERSION TEST!
YOU QUALIFY. YOU ARE FAT, DEFINITELY!
ALERT THE MEDIA!

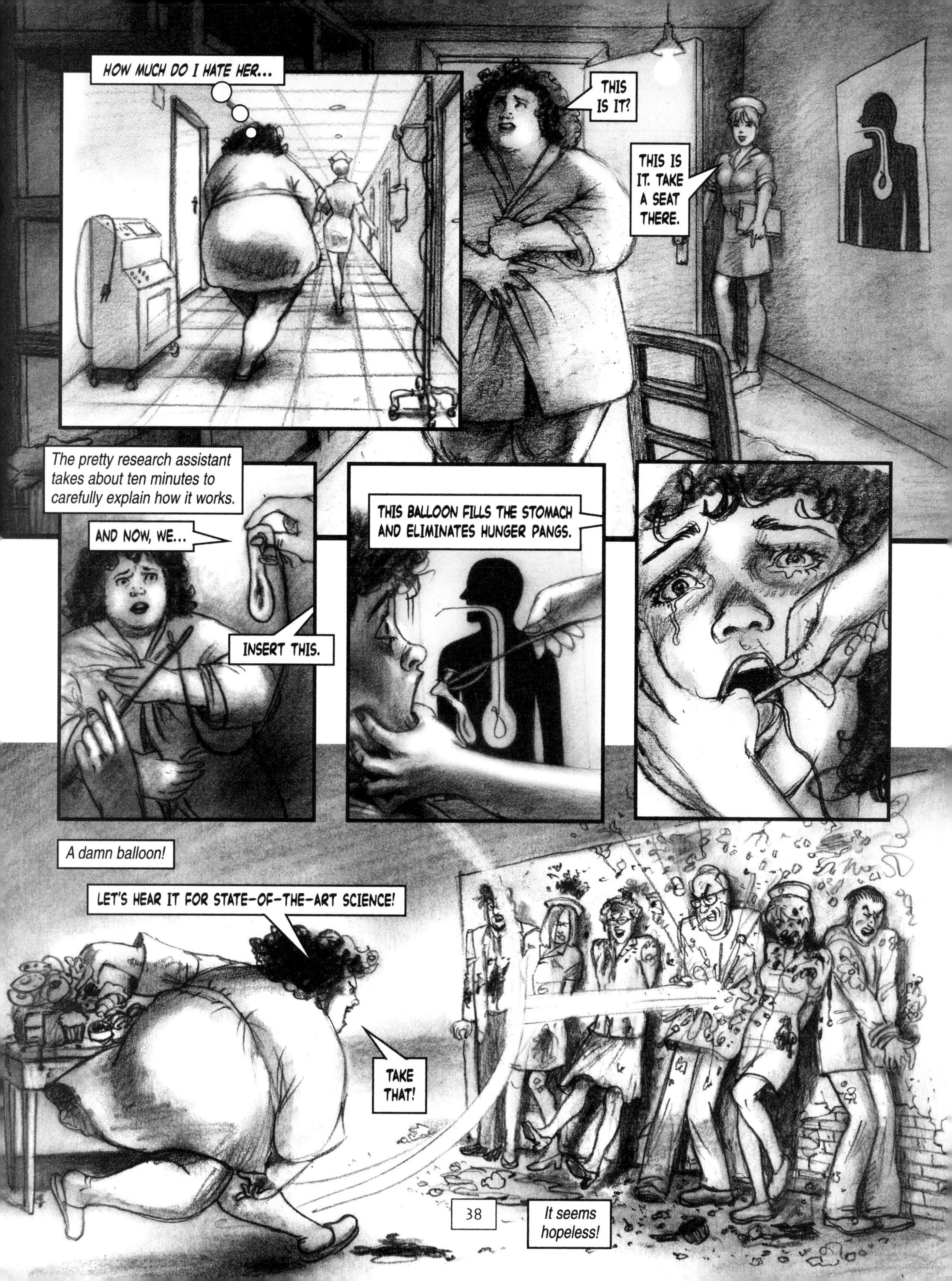
HOW MUCH DO I HATE HER...
THIS IS IT?
THIS IS IT. TAKE A SEAT THERE.
The pretty research assistant takes about ten minutes to carefully explain how it works.
AND NOW, WE...
INSERT THIS.
THIS BALLOON FILLS THE STOMACH AND ELIMINATES HUNGER PANGS.
A damn balloon!
LET'S HEAR IT FOR STATE-OF-THE-ART SCIENCE!
TAKE THAT!
It seems hopeless!

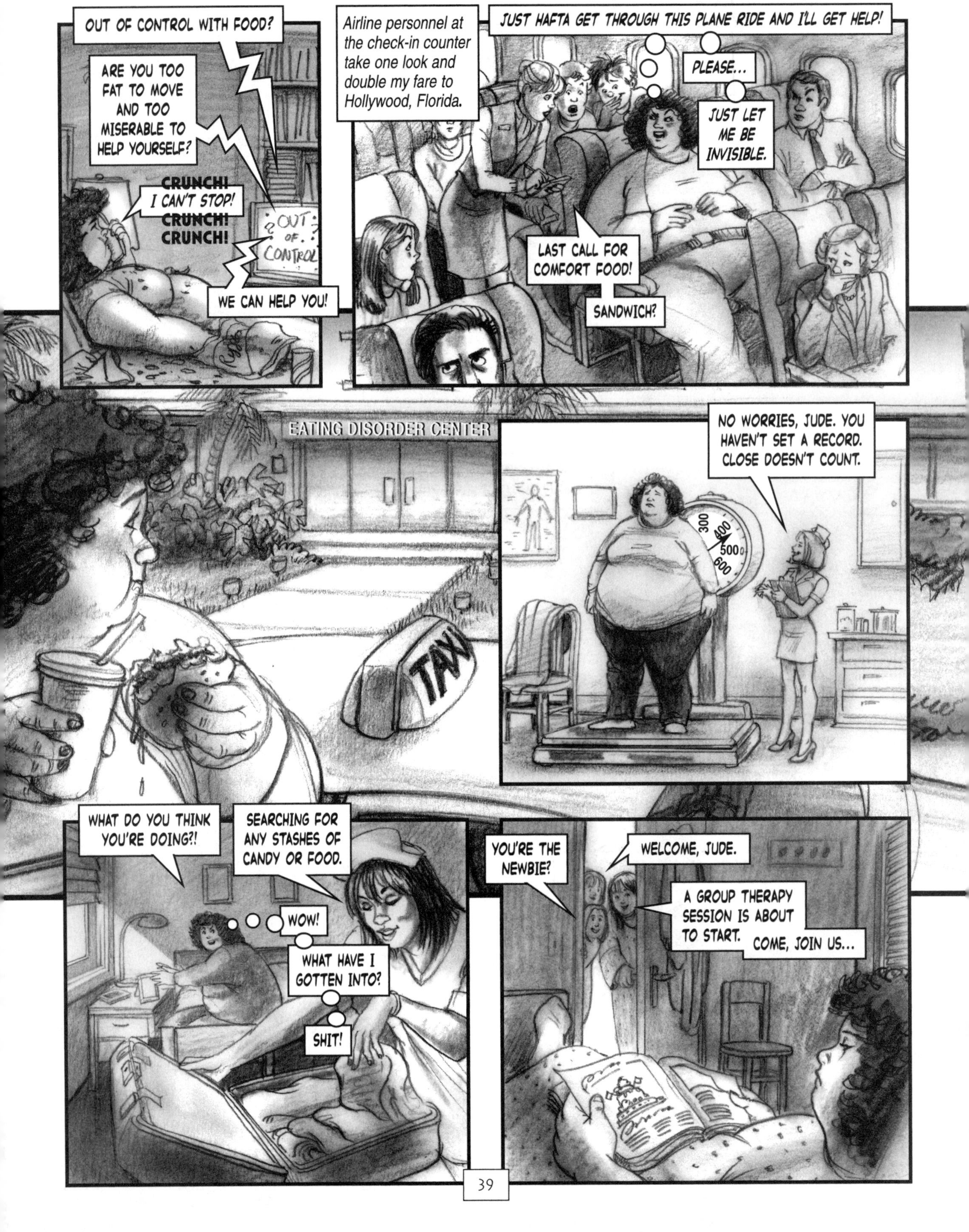

OUT OF CONTROL WITH FOOD?
ARE YOU TOO FAT TO MOVE AND TOO MISERABLE TO HELP YOURSELF?
CRUNCH!
I CAN'T STOP!
CRUNCH!
CRUNCH!
OUT OF CONTROL
WE CAN HELP YOU!
Airline personnel at the check-in counter take one look and double my fare to Hollywood, Florida.
JUST HAFTA GET THROUGH THIS PLANE RIDE AND I'LL GET HELP!
PLEASE...
JUST LET ME BE INVISIBLE.
LAST CALL FOR COMFORT FOOD!
SANDWICH?
EATING DISORDER CENTER
TAXI
NO WORRIES, JUDE. YOU HAVEN'T SET A RECORD. CLOSE DOESN'T COUNT.
300
400
500
600
WHAT DO YOU THINK YOU'RE DOING?!
SEARCHING FOR ANY STASHES OF CANDY OR FOOD.
WOW!
WHAT HAVE I GOTTEN INTO?
SHIT!
YOU'RE THE NEWBIE?
WELCOME, JUDE.
A GROUP THERAPY SESSION IS ABOUT TO START.
COME, JOIN US...

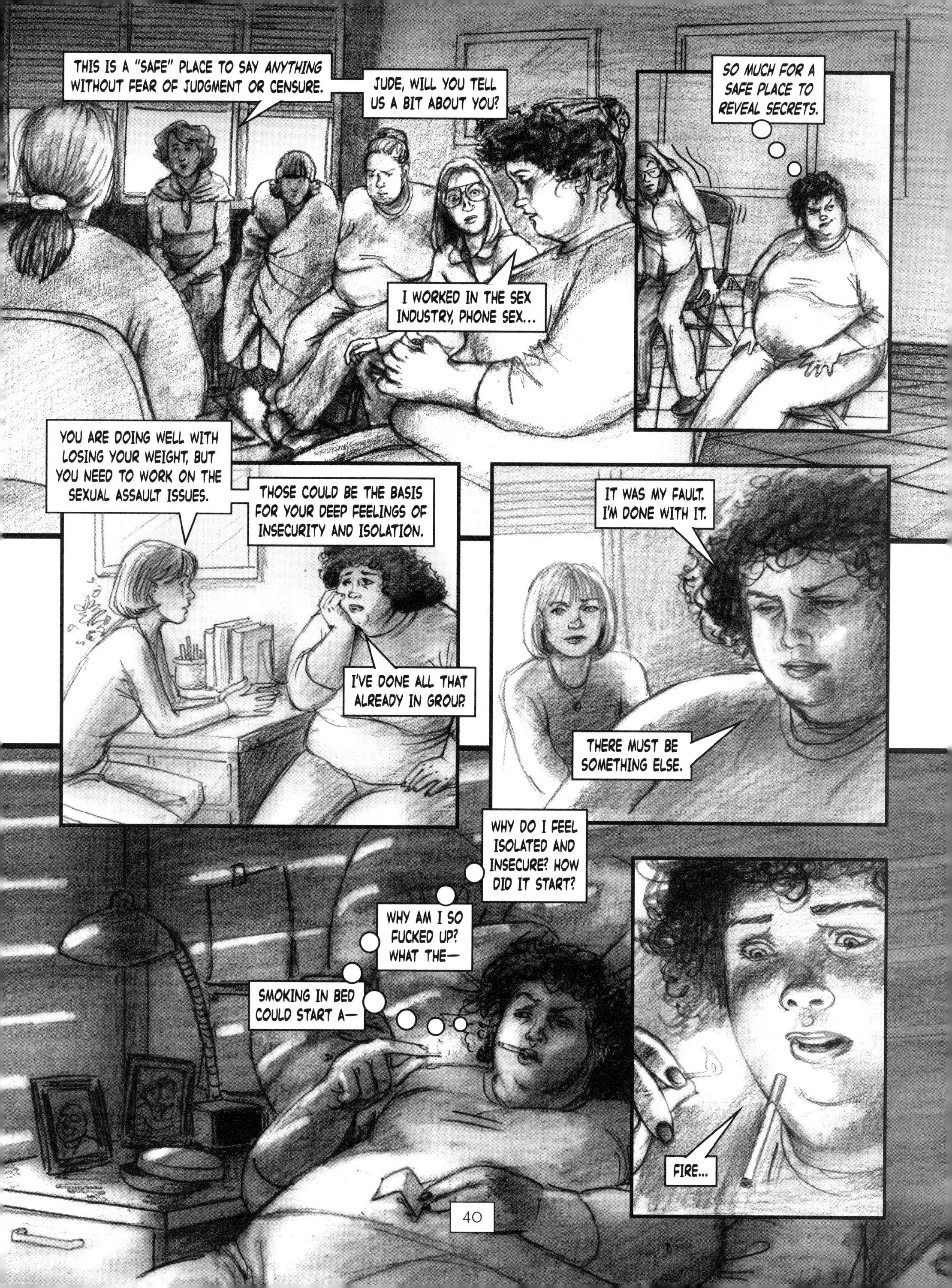
THIS IS A "SAFE" PLACE TO SAY ANYTHING WITHOUT FEAR OF JUDGMENT OR CENSURE.
JUDE, WILL YOU TELL US A BIT ABOUT YOU?
I WORKED IN THE SEX INDUSTRY, PHONE SEX...
SO MUCH FOR A SAFE PLACE TO REVEAL SECRETS.
YOU ARE DOING WELL WITH LOSING YOUR WEIGHT, BUT YOU NEED TO WORK ON THE SEXUAL ASSAULT ISSUES.
THOSE COULD BE THE BASIS FOR YOUR DEEP FEELINGS OF INSECURITY AND ISOLATION.
I'VE DONE ALL THAT ALREADY IN GROUP.
IT WAS MY FAULT. I'M DONE WITH IT.
THERE MUST BE SOMETHING ELSE.
WHY DO I FEEL ISOLATED AND INSECURE? HOW DID IT START?
WHY AM I SO FUCKED UP? WHAT THE—
SMOKING IN BED COULD START A—
FIRE...

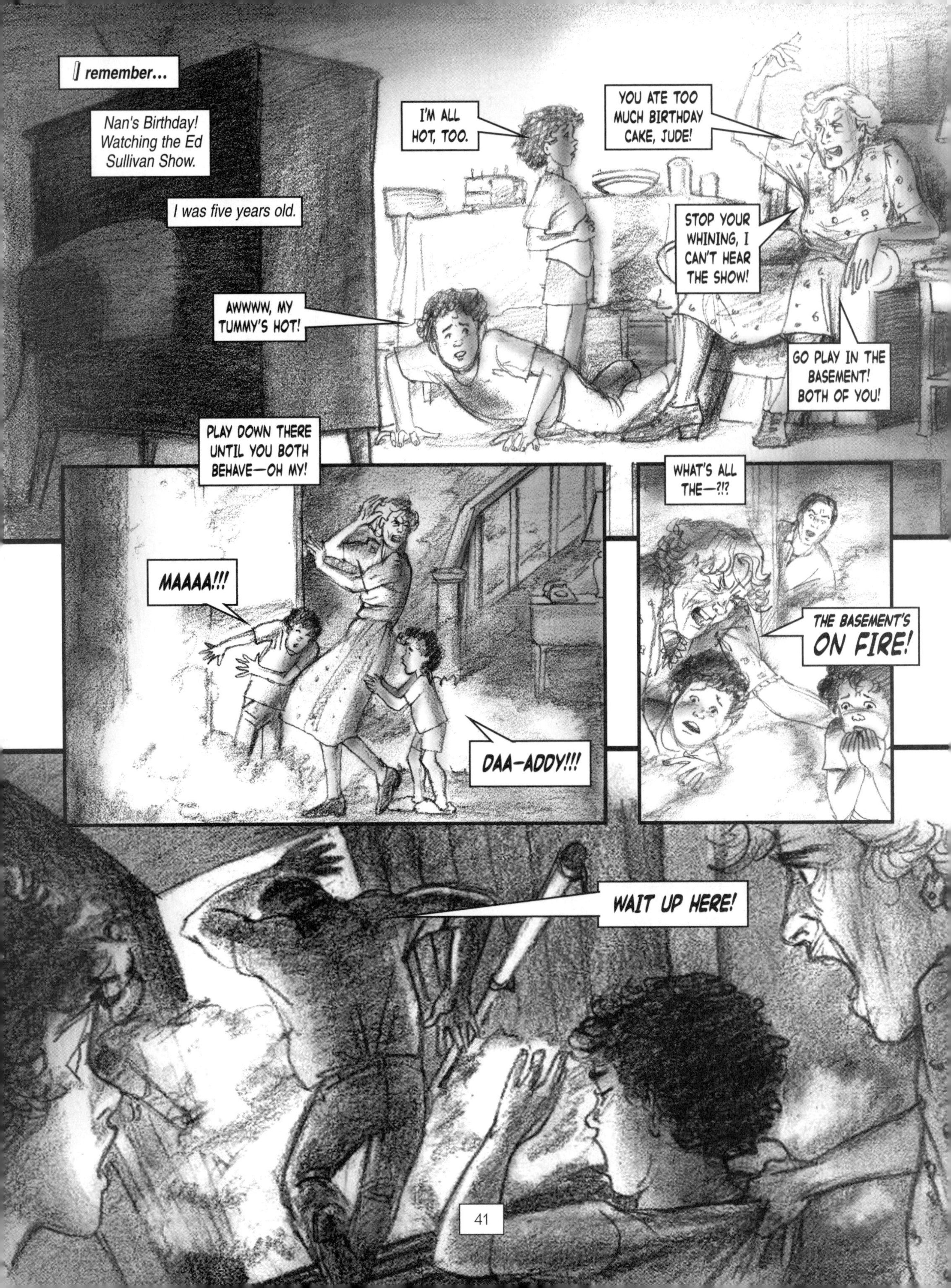
I remember...
Nan's Birthday! Watching the Ed Sullivan Show.
I was five years old.
I'M ALL HOT, TOO.
YOU ATE TOO MUCH BIRTHDAY CAKE, JUDE!
STOP YOUR WHINING, I CAN'T HEAR THE SHOW!
AWWWW, MY TUMMY'S HOT!
GO PLAY IN THE BASEMENT! BOTH OF YOU!
PLAY DOWN THERE UNTIL YOU BOTH BEHAVE—OH MY!
MAAAA!!!
DAA-ADDY!!!
WHAT'S ALL THE—?!?
THE BASEMENT'S ON FIRE!
WAIT UP HERE!

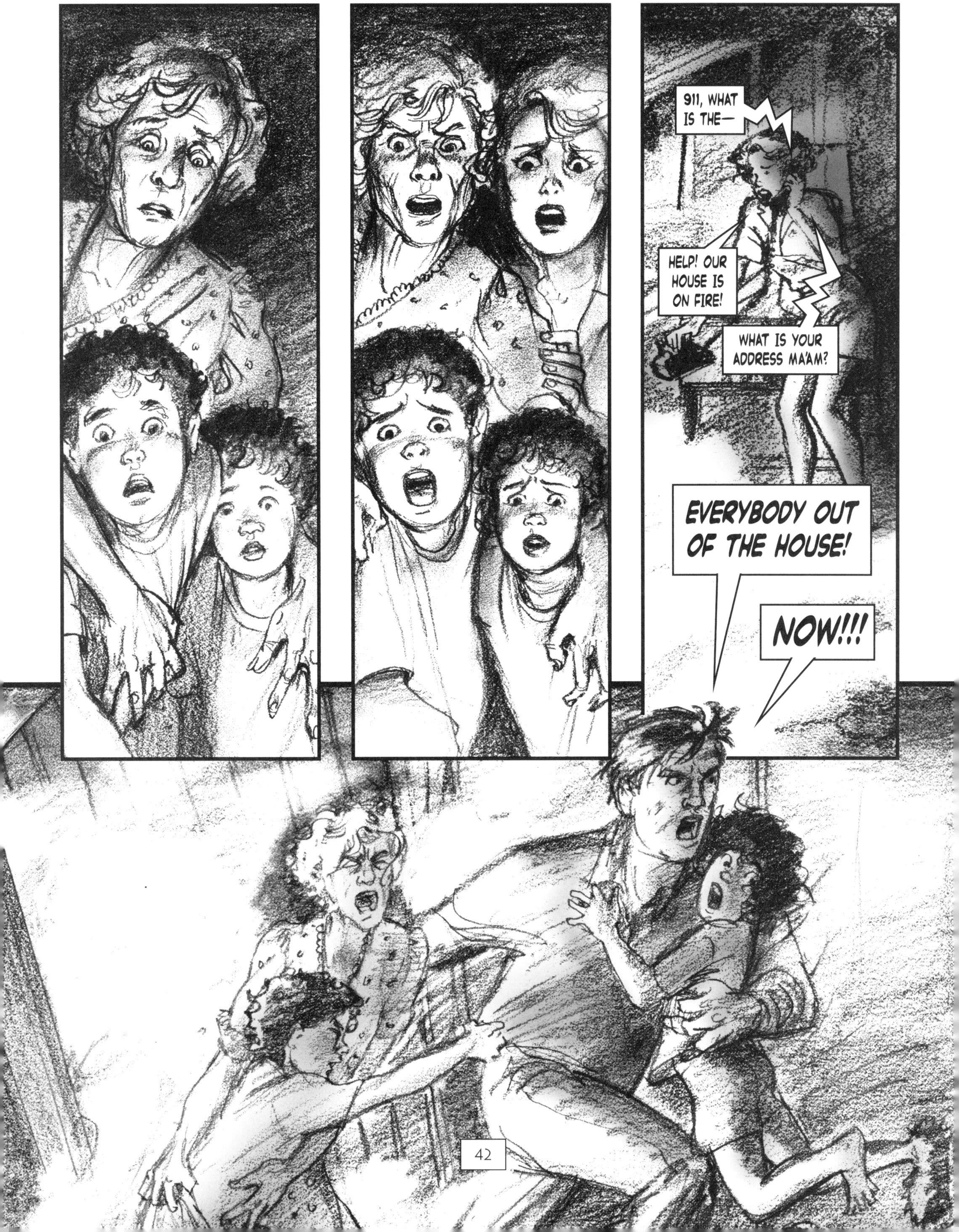
911, WHAT IS THE—
HELP! OUR HOUSE IS ON FIRE!
WHAT IS YOUR ADDRESS MA'AM?
EVERYBODY OUT OF THE HOUSE!
NOW!!!

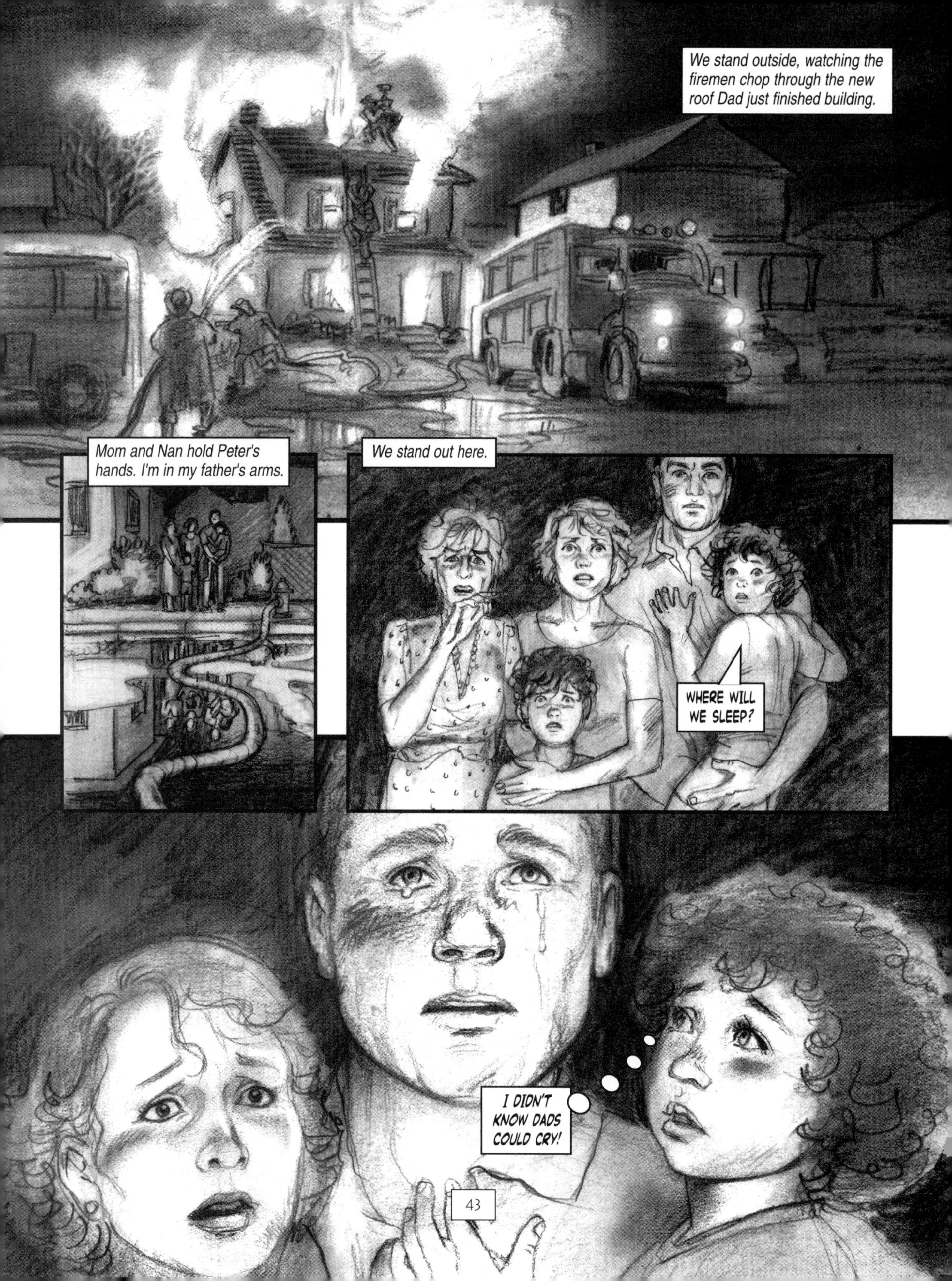
We stand outside, watching the firemen chop through the new roof Dad just finished building.
Mom and Nan hold Peter's hands. I'm in my father's arms.
We stand out here.
WHERE WILL WE SLEEP?
I DIDN'T KNOW DADS COULD CRY!

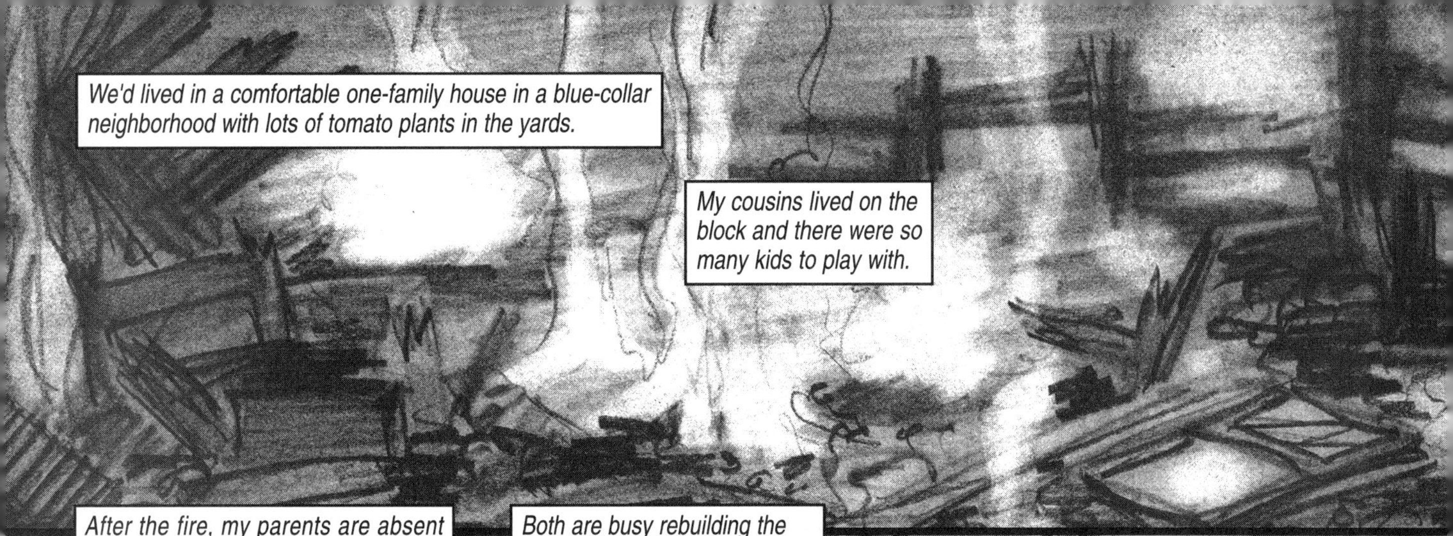
We'd lived in a comfortable one-family house in a blue-collar neighborhood with lots of tomato plants in the yards.
My cousins lived on the block and there were so many kids to play with.

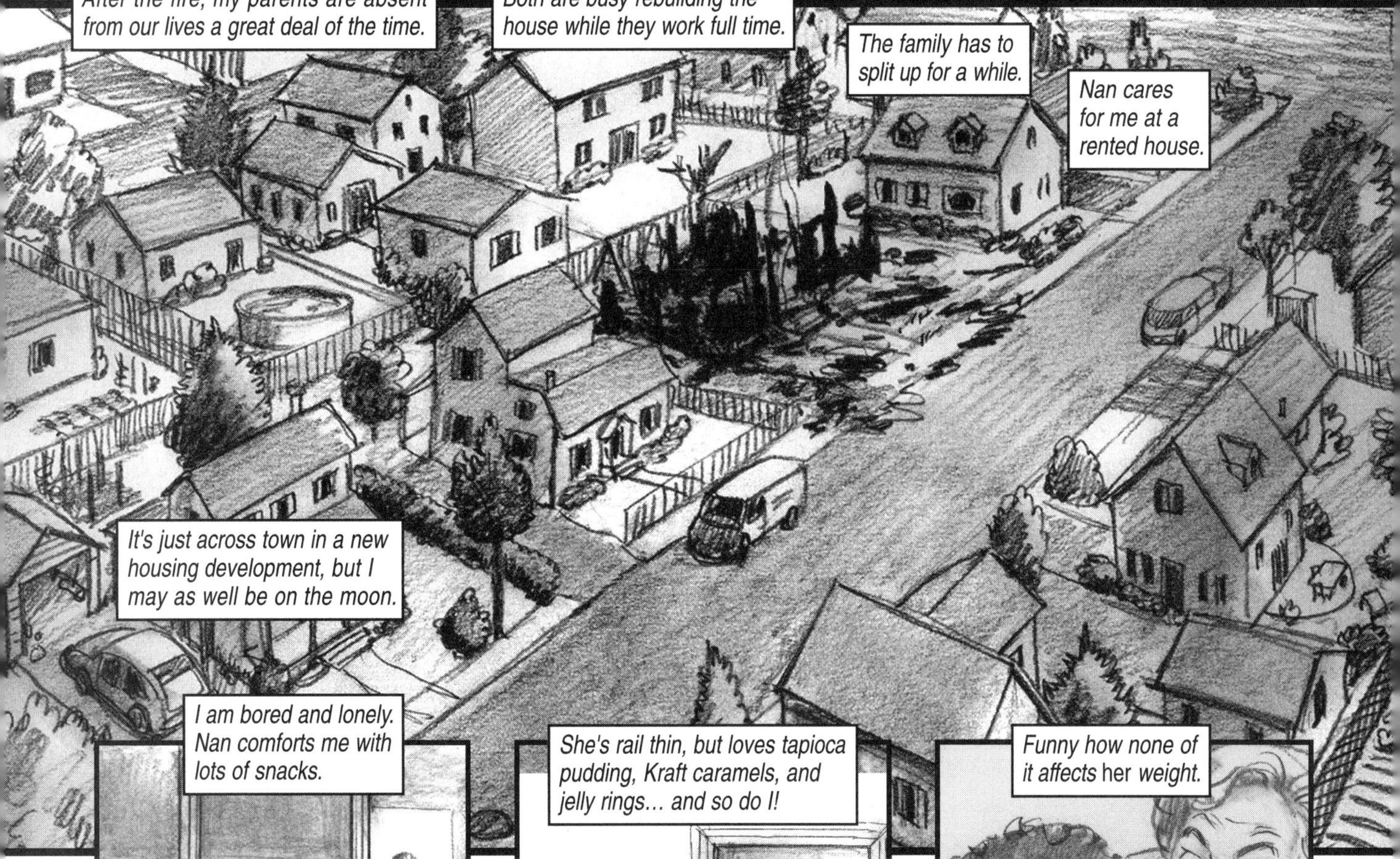
After the fire, my parents are absent from our lives a great deal of the time.
Both are busy rebuilding the house while they work full time.
The family has to split up for a while.
Nan cares for me at a rented house.
It's just across town in a new housing development, but I may as well be on the moon.

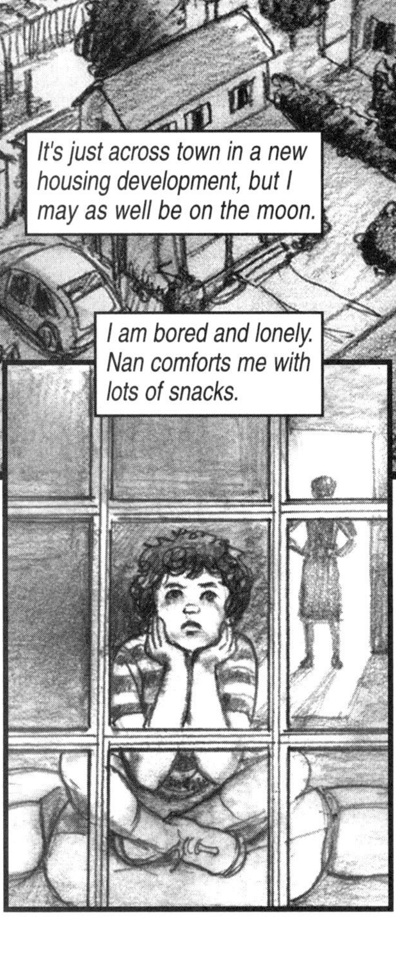
I am bored and lonely. Nan comforts me with lots of snacks.

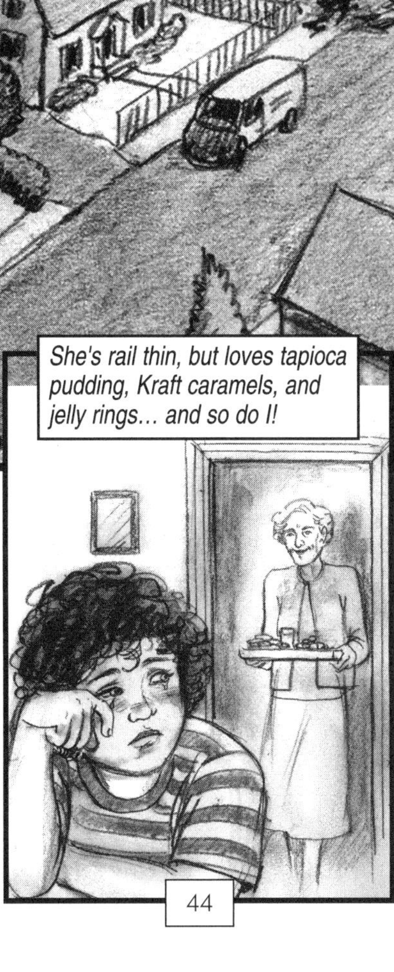
She's rail thin, but loves tapioca pudding, Kraft caramels, and jelly rings… and so do I!

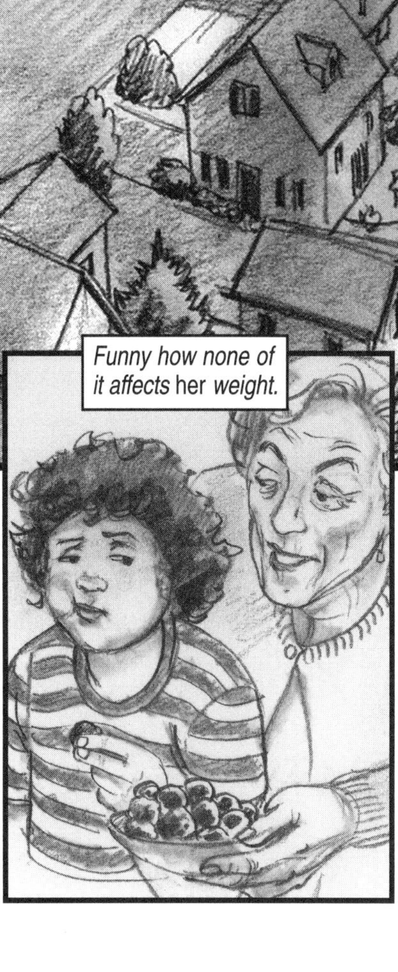
Funny how none of it affects her weight.

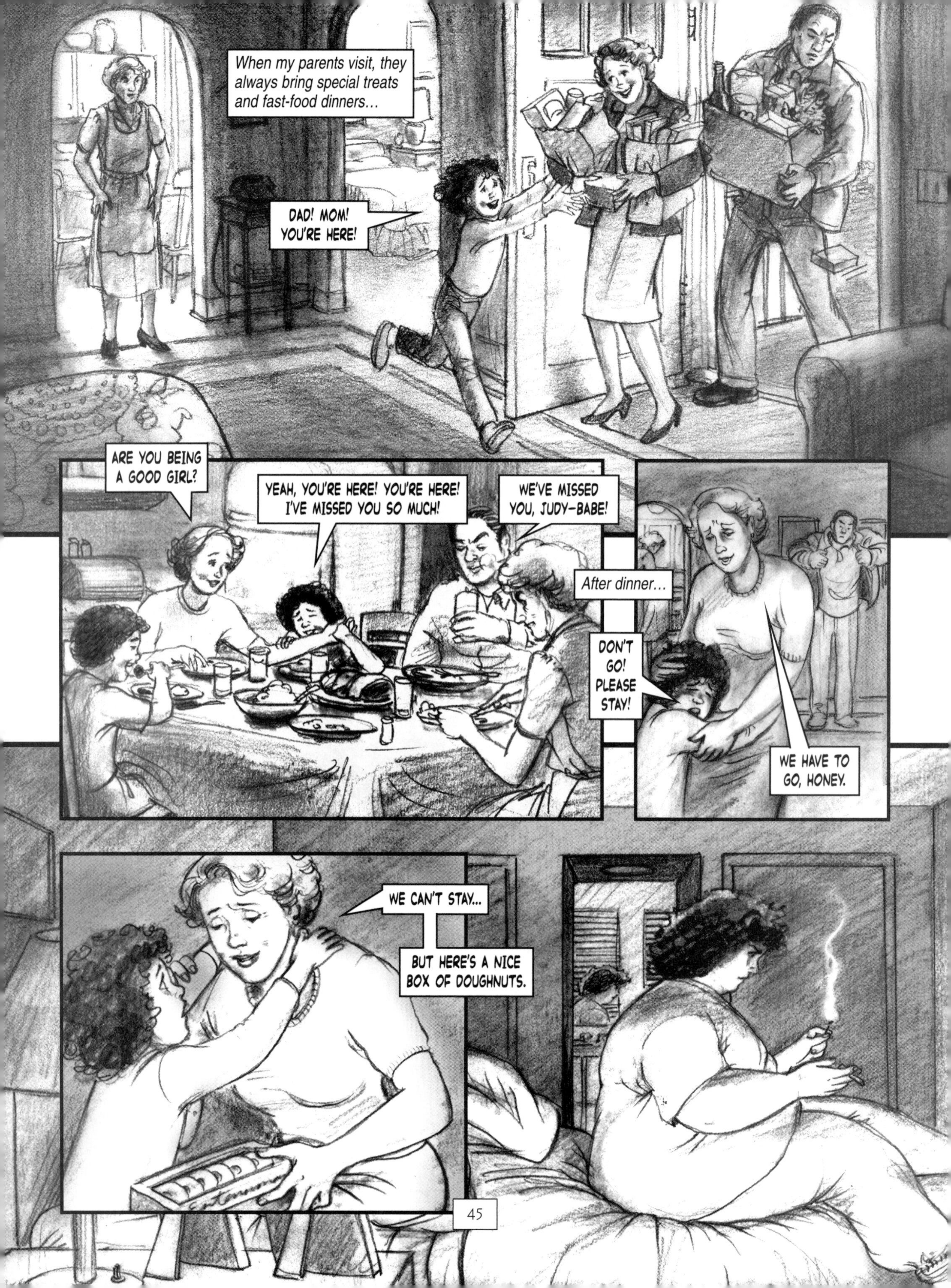
When my parents visit, they always bring special treats and fast-food dinners…
DAD! MOM! YOU'RE HERE!
ARE YOU BEING A GOOD GIRL?
YEAH, YOU'RE HERE! YOU'RE HERE! I'VE MISSED YOU SO MUCH!
WE'VE MISSED YOU, JUDY-BABE!
After dinner…
DON'T GO! PLEASE STAY!
WE HAVE TO GO, HONEY.
WE CAN'T STAY…
BUT HERE'S A NICE BOX OF DOUGHNUTS.

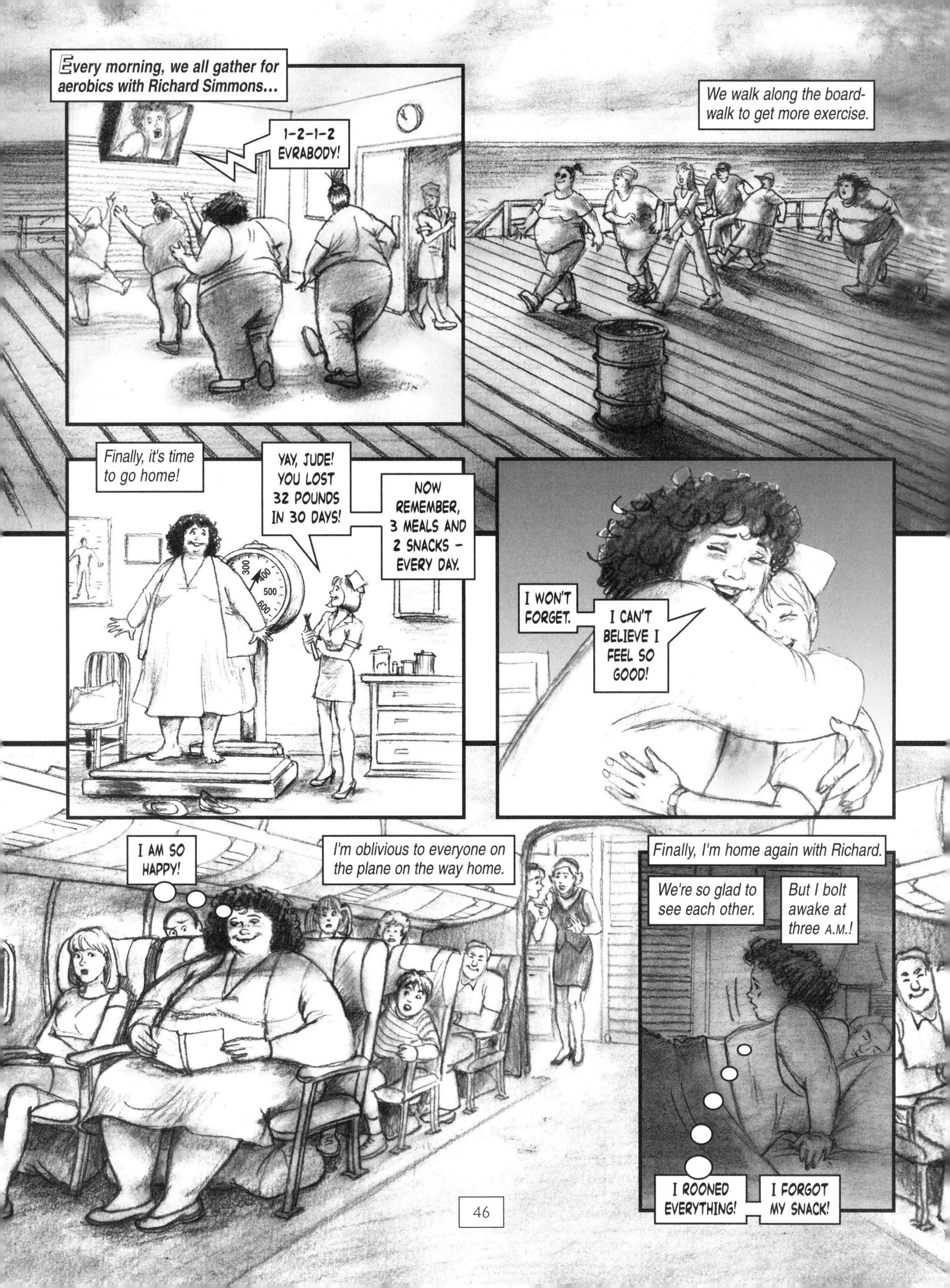
Every morning, we all gather for aerobics with Richard Simmons…
1-2-1-2 EVRABODY!
We walk along the boardwalk to get more exercise.
Finally, it's time to go home!
YAY, JUDE! YOU LOST 32 POUNDS IN 30 DAYS!
NOW REMEMBER, 3 MEALS AND 2 SNACKS – EVERY DAY.
300
400
500
600
I WON'T FORGET.
I CAN'T BELIEVE I FEEL SO GOOD!
I AM SO HAPPY!
I'm oblivious to everyone on the plane on the way home.
Finally, I'm home again with Richard.
We're so glad to see each other.
But I bolt awake at three A.M.!
I ROONED EVERYTHING!
I FORGOT MY SNACK!

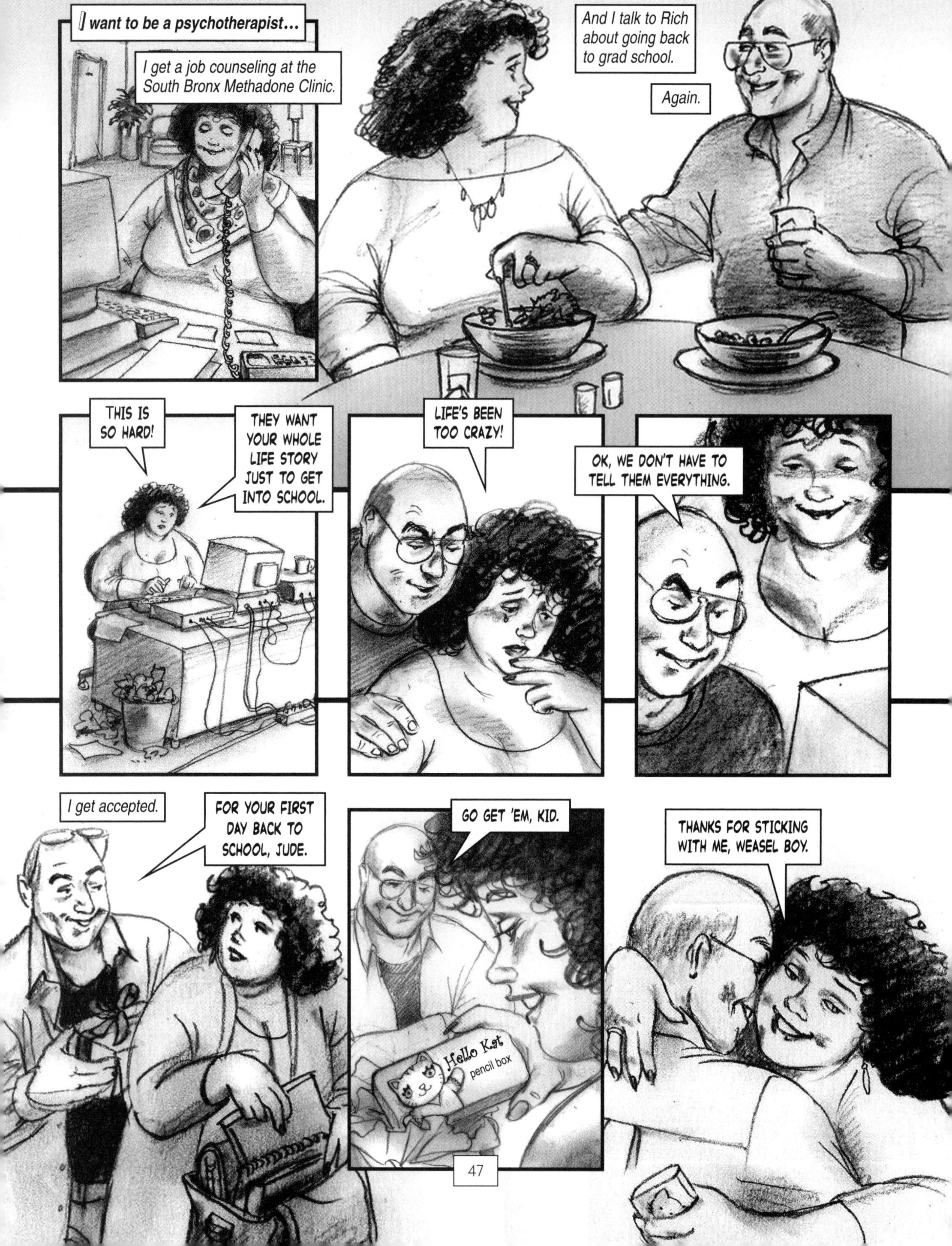
I want to be a psychotherapist…
I get a job counseling at the South Bronx Methadone Clinic.
And I talk to Rich about going back to grad school.
Again.
THIS IS SO HARD!
THEY WANT YOUR WHOLE LIFE STORY JUST TO GET INTO SCHOOL.
LIFE'S BEEN TOO CRAZY!
OK, WE DON'T HAVE TO TELL THEM EVERYTHING.
I get accepted.
FOR YOUR FIRST DAY BACK TO SCHOOL, JUDE.
GO GET 'EM, KID.
Hello Kat
pencil box
THANKS FOR STICKING WITH ME, WEASEL BOY.

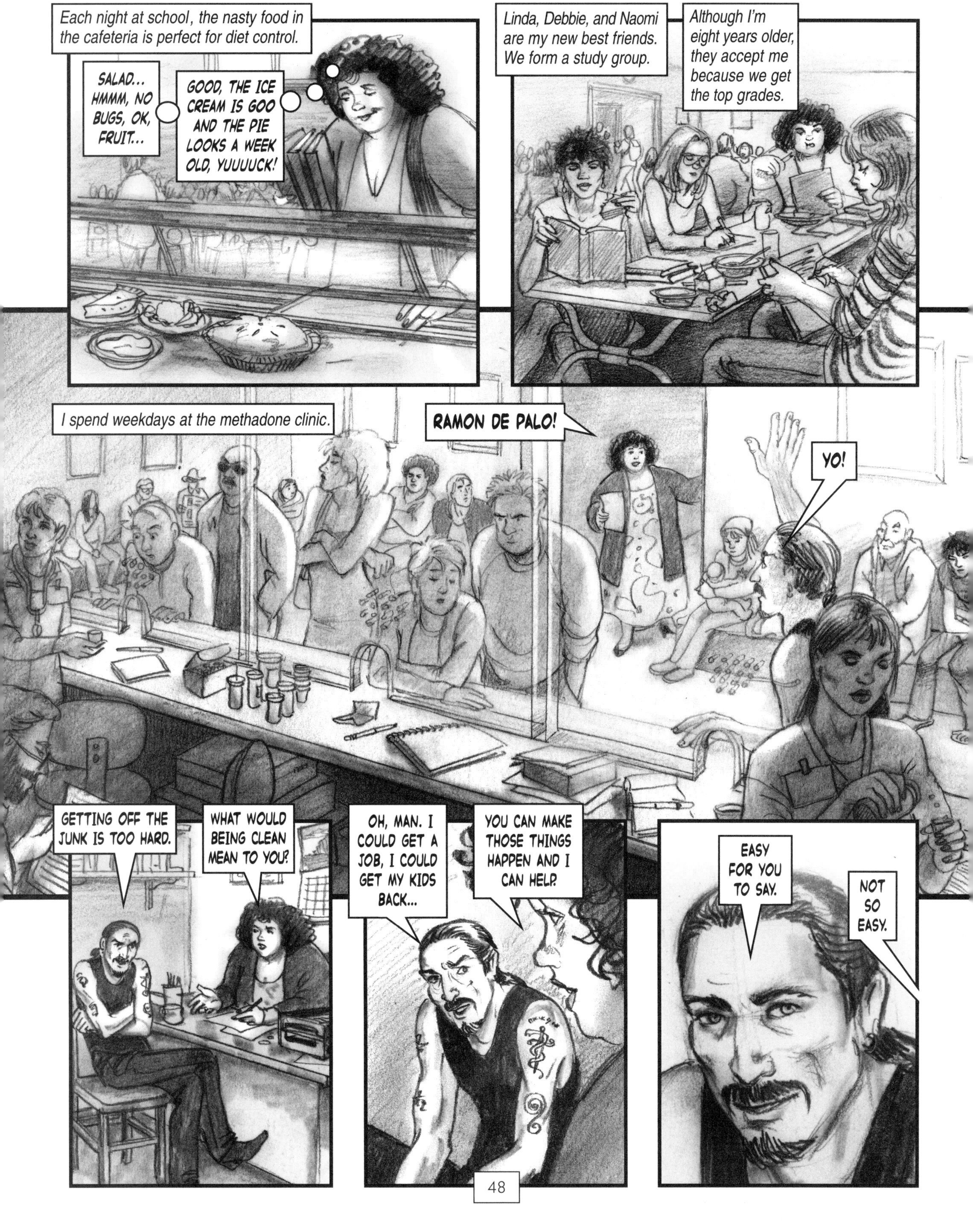
Each night at school, the nasty food in the cafeteria is perfect for diet control.
SALAD... HMMM, NO BUGS, OK, FRUIT...
GOOD, THE ICE CREAM IS GOO AND THE PIE LOOKS A WEEK OLD, YUUUUCK!
Linda, Debbie, and Naomi are my new best friends. We form a study group.
Although I'm eight years older, they accept me because we get the top grades.
I spend weekdays at the methadone clinic.
RAMON DE PALO!
YO!
GETTING OFF THE JUNK IS TOO HARD.
WHAT WOULD BEING CLEAN MEAN TO YOU?
OH, MAN. I COULD GET A JOB, I COULD GET MY KIDS BACK...
YOU CAN MAKE THOSE THINGS HAPPEN AND I CAN HELP.
EASY FOR YOU TO SAY.
NOT SO EASY.

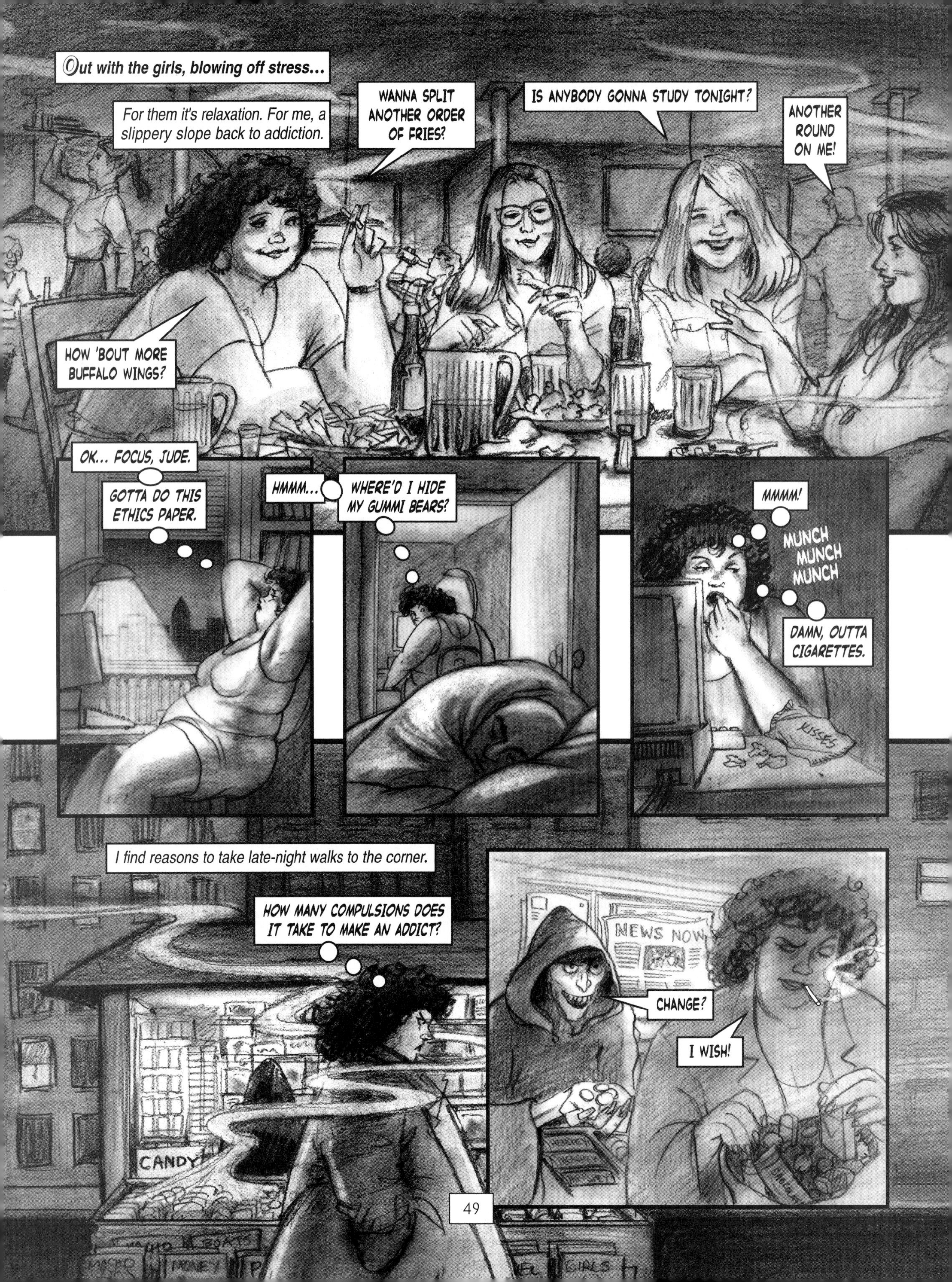
Out with the girls, blowing off stress...
For them it's relaxation. For me, a slippery slope back to addiction.
WANNA SPLIT ANOTHER ORDER OF FRIES?
IS ANYBODY GONNA STUDY TONIGHT?
ANOTHER ROUND ON ME!
HOW 'BOUT MORE BUFFALO WINGS?
OK... FOCUS, JUDE.
GOTTA DO THIS ETHICS PAPER.
HMMM...
WHERE'D I HIDE MY GUMMI BEARS?
MMMM!
MUNCH MUNCH MUNCH
DAMN, OUTTA CIGARETTES.
KISSES
I find reasons to take late-night walks to the corner.
HOW MANY COMPULSIONS DOES IT TAKE TO MAKE AN ADDICT?
CANDY
NEWS NOW
CHANGE?
I WISH!
MONEY
GIRLS

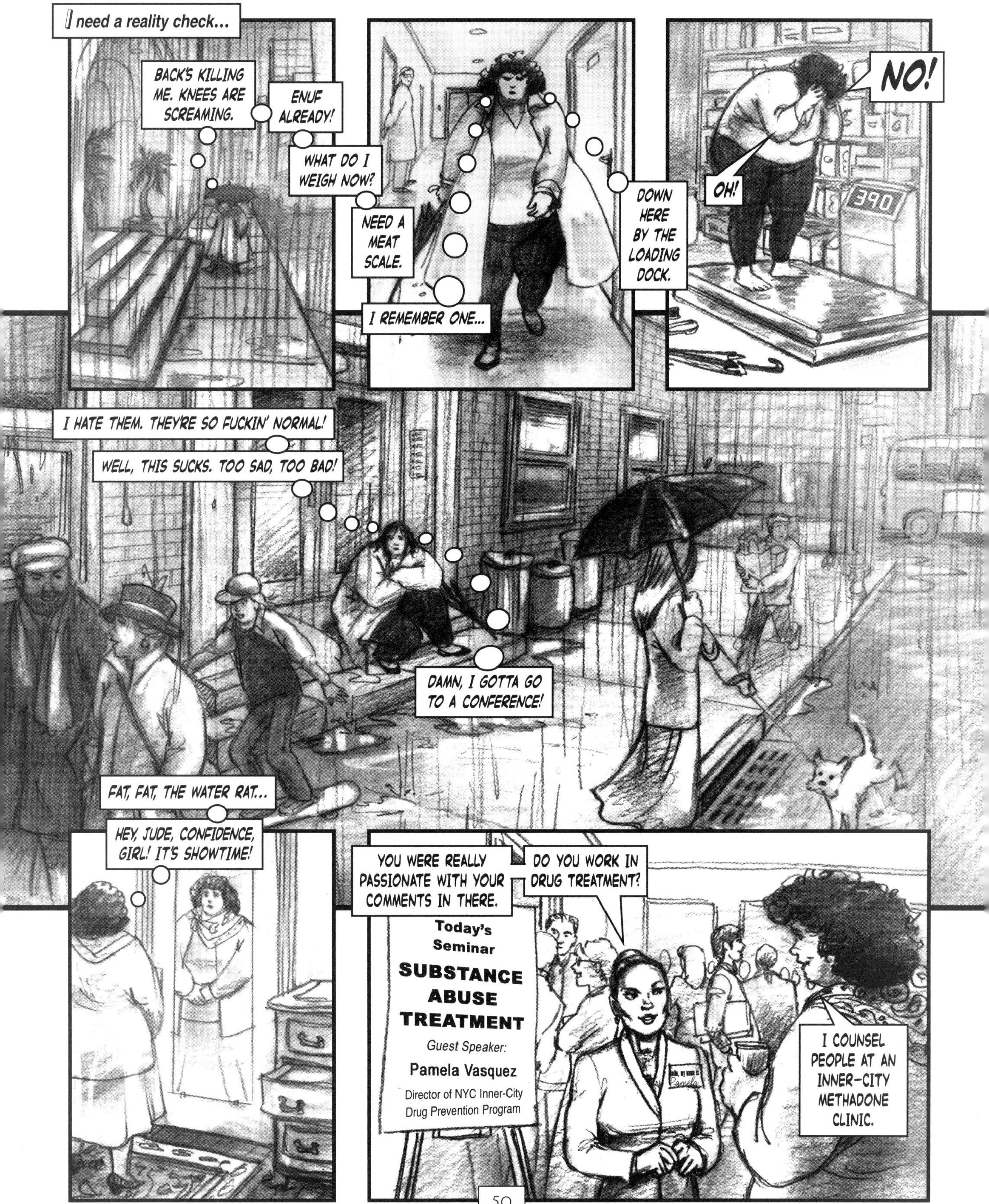
I need a reality check...
BACK'S KILLING ME. KNEES ARE SCREAMING.
ENUF ALREADY!
WHAT DO I WEIGH NOW?
NEED A MEAT SCALE.
I REMEMBER ONE...
DOWN HERE BY THE LOADING DOCK.
NO!
OH!
390
I HATE THEM. THEY'RE SO FUCKIN' NORMAL!
WELL, THIS SUCKS. TOO SAD, TOO BAD!
DAMN, I GOTTA GO TO A CONFERENCE!
FAT, FAT, THE WATER RAT...
HEY, JUDE, CONFIDENCE, GIRL! IT'S SHOWTIME!
YOU WERE REALLY PASSIONATE WITH YOUR COMMENTS IN THERE.
DO YOU WORK IN DRUG TREATMENT?
Today's Seminar
SUBSTANCE ABUSE TREATMENT
Guest Speaker:
Pamela Vasquez
Director of NYC Inner-City Drug Prevention Program
I COUNSEL PEOPLE AT AN INNER-CITY METHADONE CLINIC.

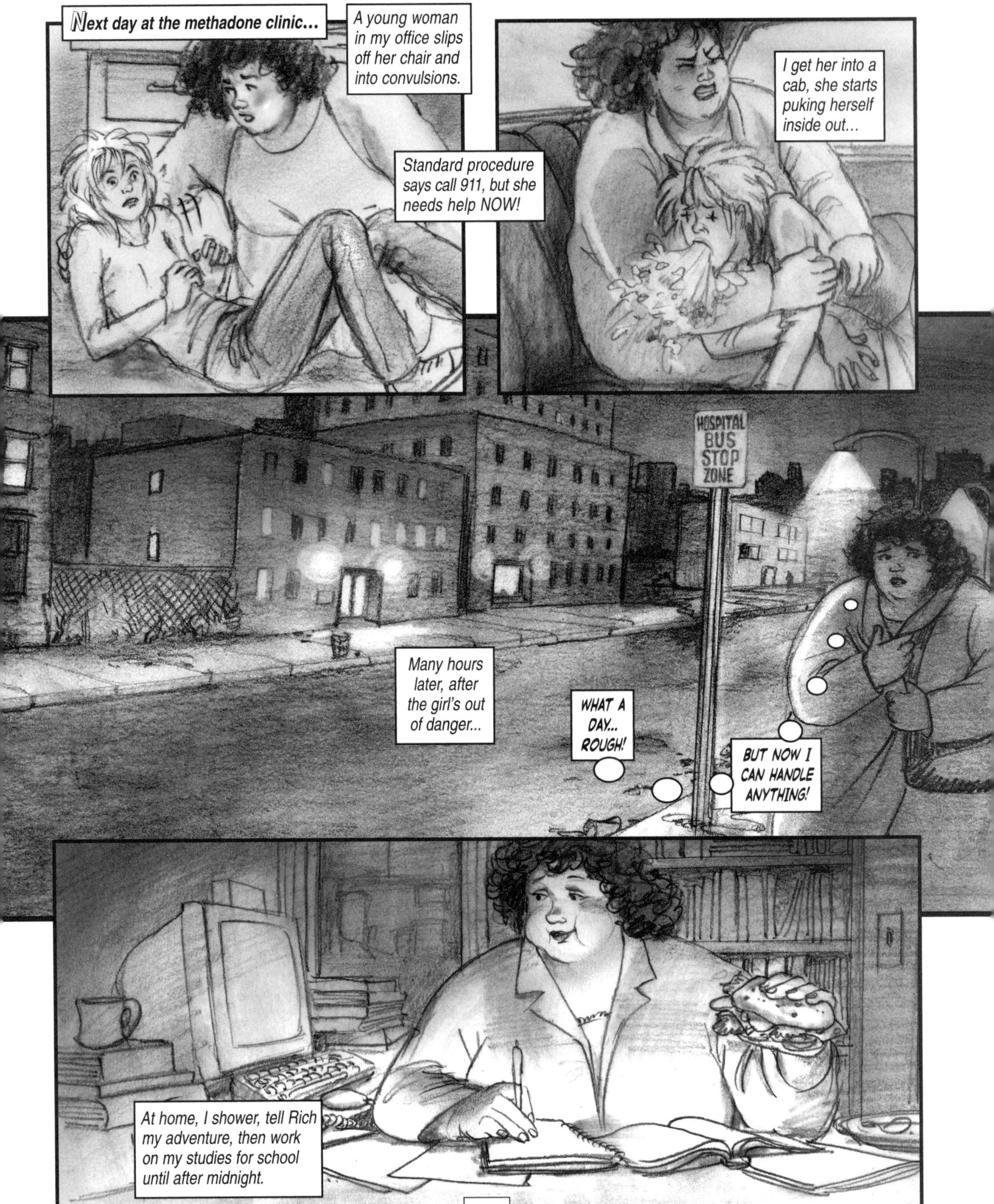
Next day at the methadone clinic…
A young woman in my office slips off her chair and into convulsions.
Standard procedure says call 911, but she needs help NOW!
I get her into a cab, she starts puking herself inside out…
HOSPITAL BUS STOP ZONE
Many hours later, after the girl's out of danger...
WHAT A DAY... ROUGH!
BUT NOW I CAN HANDLE ANYTHING!
At home, I shower, tell Rich my adventure, then work on my studies for school until after midnight.

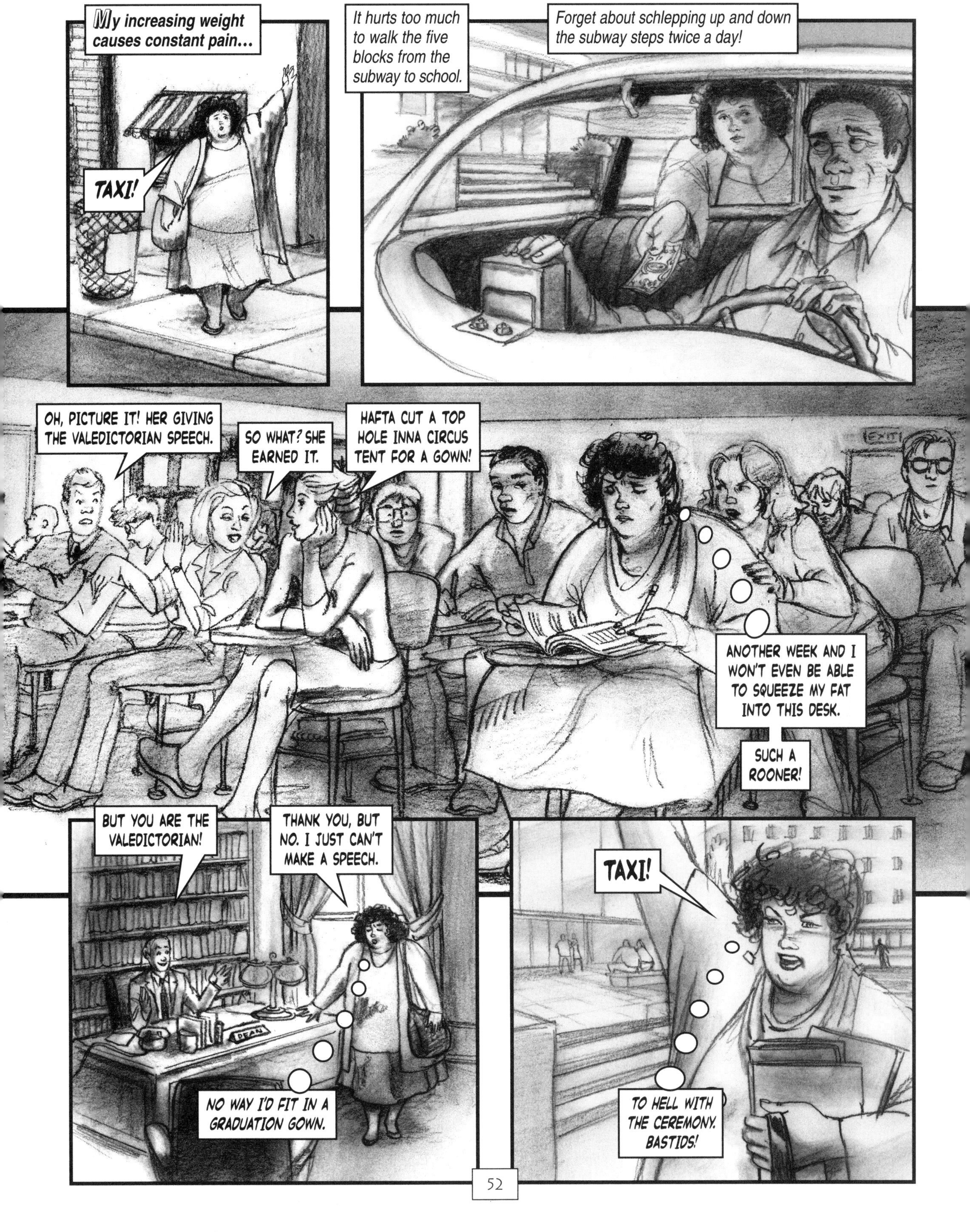
My increasing weight causes constant pain…
TAXI!
It hurts too much to walk the five blocks from the subway to school.
Forget about schlepping up and down the subway steps twice a day!
OH, PICTURE IT! HER GIVING THE VALEDICTORIAN SPEECH.
SO WHAT? SHE EARNED IT.
HAFTA CUT A TOP HOLE INNA CIRCUS TENT FOR A GOWN!
ANOTHER WEEK AND I WON'T EVEN BE ABLE TO SQUEEZE MY FAT INTO THIS DESK.
SUCH A ROONER!
BUT YOU ARE THE VALEDICTORIAN!
THANK YOU, BUT NO. I JUST CAN'T MAKE A SPEECH.
NO WAY I'D FIT IN A GRADUATION GOWN.
TAXI!
TO HELL WITH THE CEREMONY. BASTIDS!

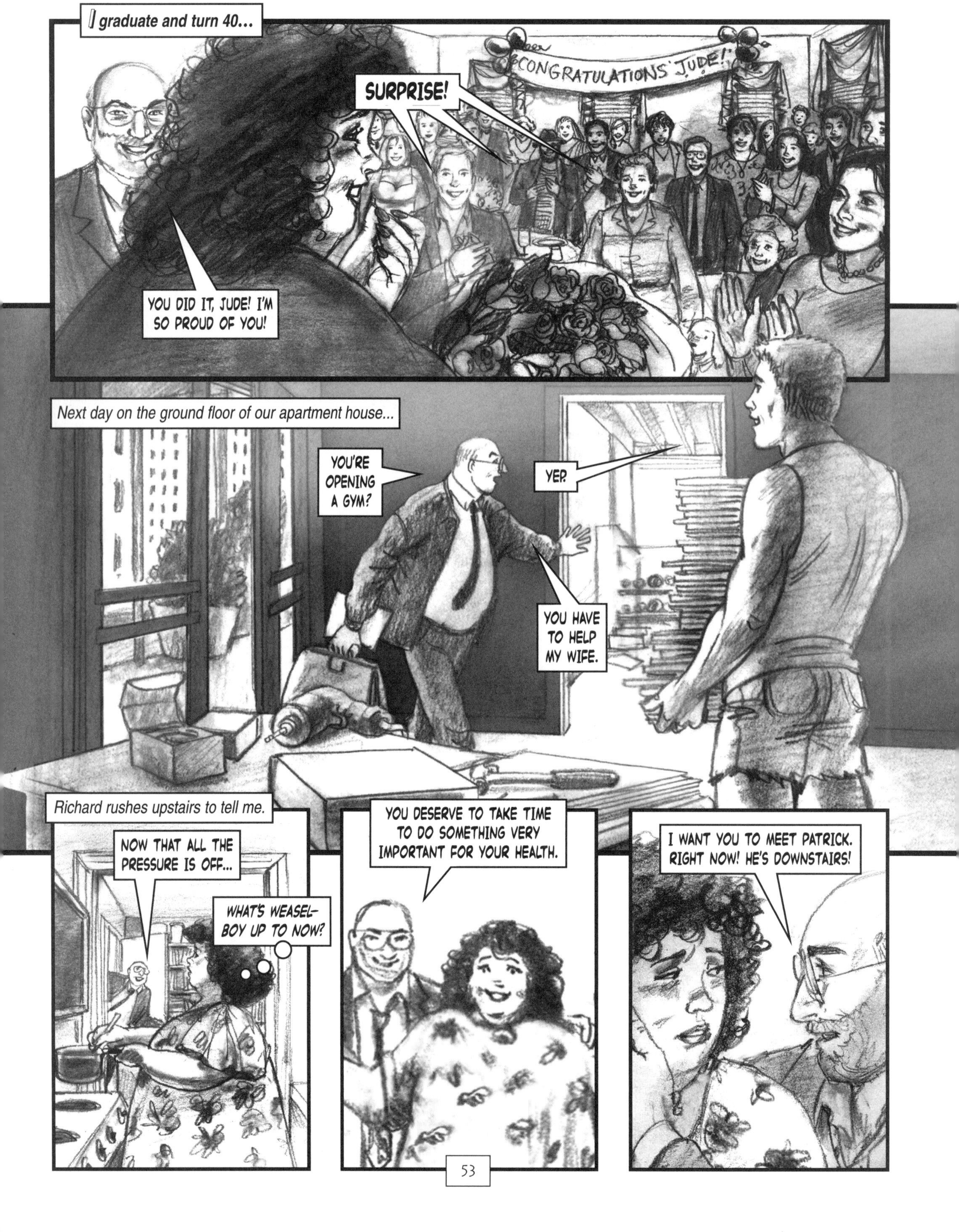

I graduate and turn 40…
CONGRATULATIONS JUDE!
SURPRISE!
YOU DID IT, JUDE! I'M SO PROUD OF YOU!
Next day on the ground floor of our apartment house...
YOU'RE OPENING A GYM?
YEP.
YOU HAVE TO HELP MY WIFE.
Richard rushes upstairs to tell me.
NOW THAT ALL THE PRESSURE IS OFF...
WHAT'S WEASEL-BOY UP TO NOW?
YOU DESERVE TO TAKE TIME TO DO SOMETHING VERY IMPORTANT FOR YOUR HEALTH.
I WANT YOU TO MEET PATRICK. RIGHT NOW! HE'S DOWNSTAIRS!

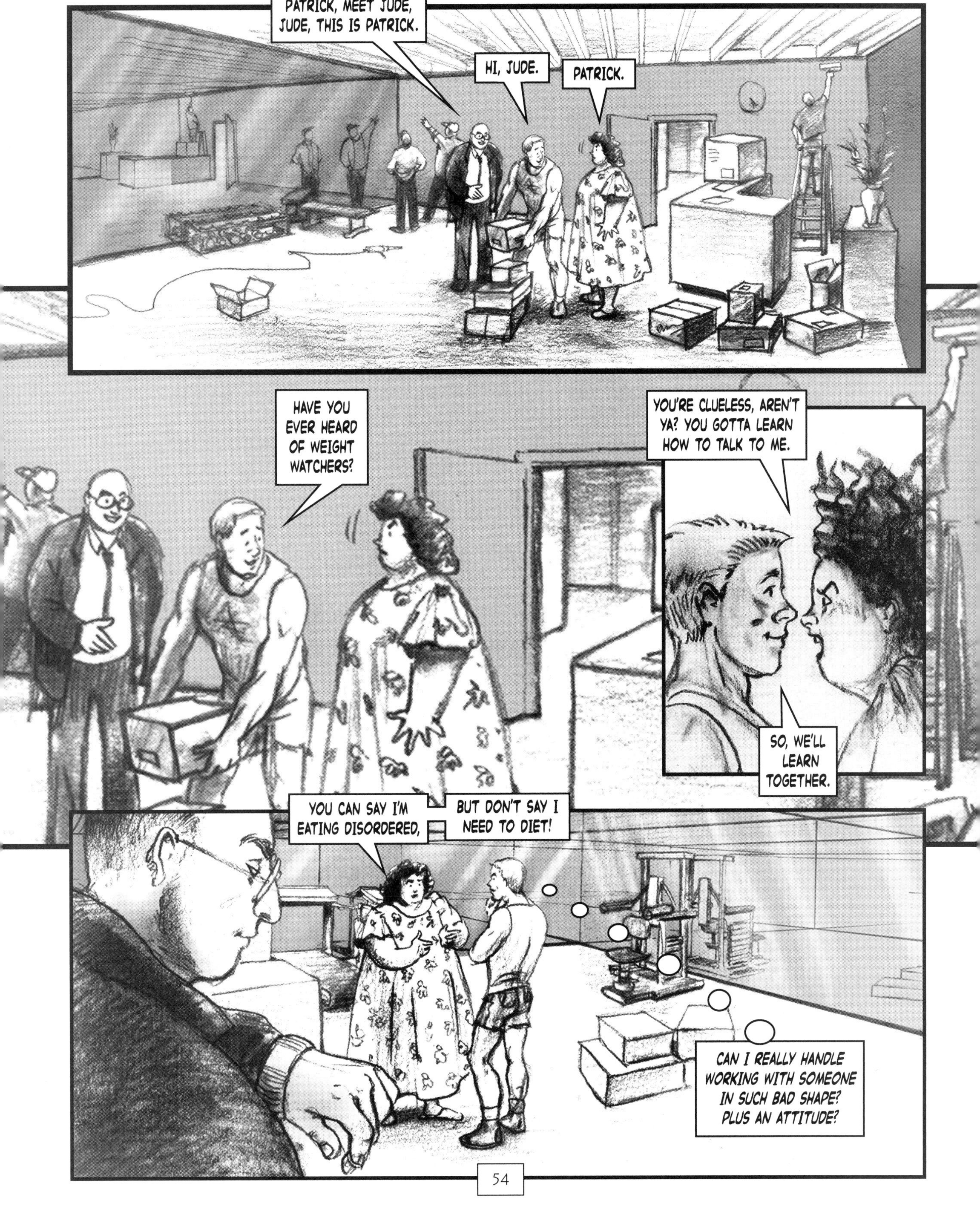
PATRICK, MEET JUDE, JUDE, THIS IS PATRICK.
HI, JUDE.
PATRICK.
HAVE YOU EVER HEARD OF WEIGHT WATCHERS?
YOU'RE CLUELESS, AREN'T YA? YOU GOTTA LEARN HOW TO TALK TO ME.
SO, WE'LL LEARN TOGETHER.
YOU CAN SAY I'M EATING DISORDERED,
BUT DON'T SAY I NEED TO DIET!
CAN I REALLY HANDLE WORKING WITH SOMEONE IN SUCH BAD SHAPE? PLUS AN ATTITUDE?

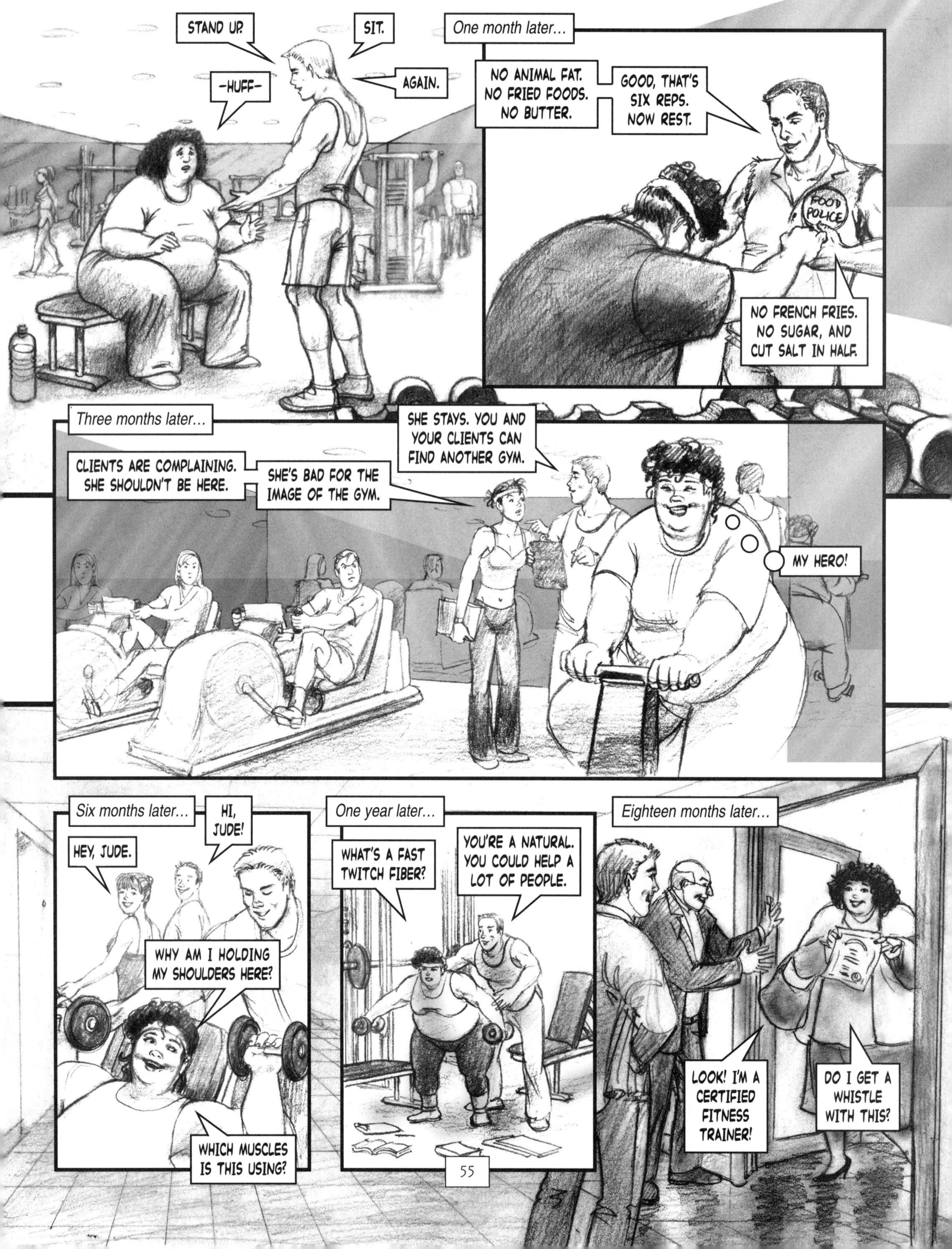
STAND UP.
-HUFF-
SIT.
AGAIN.
One month later…
NO ANIMAL FAT. NO FRIED FOODS. NO BUTTER.
GOOD, THAT'S SIX REPS. NOW REST.
FOOD POLICE
NO FRENCH FRIES. NO SUGAR, AND CUT SALT IN HALF.
Three months later…
CLIENTS ARE COMPLAINING. SHE SHOULDN'T BE HERE.
SHE'S BAD FOR THE IMAGE OF THE GYM.
SHE STAYS. YOU AND YOUR CLIENTS CAN FIND ANOTHER GYM.
MY HERO!
Six months later…
HEY, JUDE.
HI, JUDE!
WHY AM I HOLDING MY SHOULDERS HERE?
WHICH MUSCLES IS THIS USING?
One year later…
WHAT'S A FAST TWITCH FIBER?
YOU'RE A NATURAL. YOU COULD HELP A LOT OF PEOPLE.
Eighteen months later…
LOOK! I'M A CERTIFIED FITNESS TRAINER!
DO I GET A WHISTLE WITH THIS?

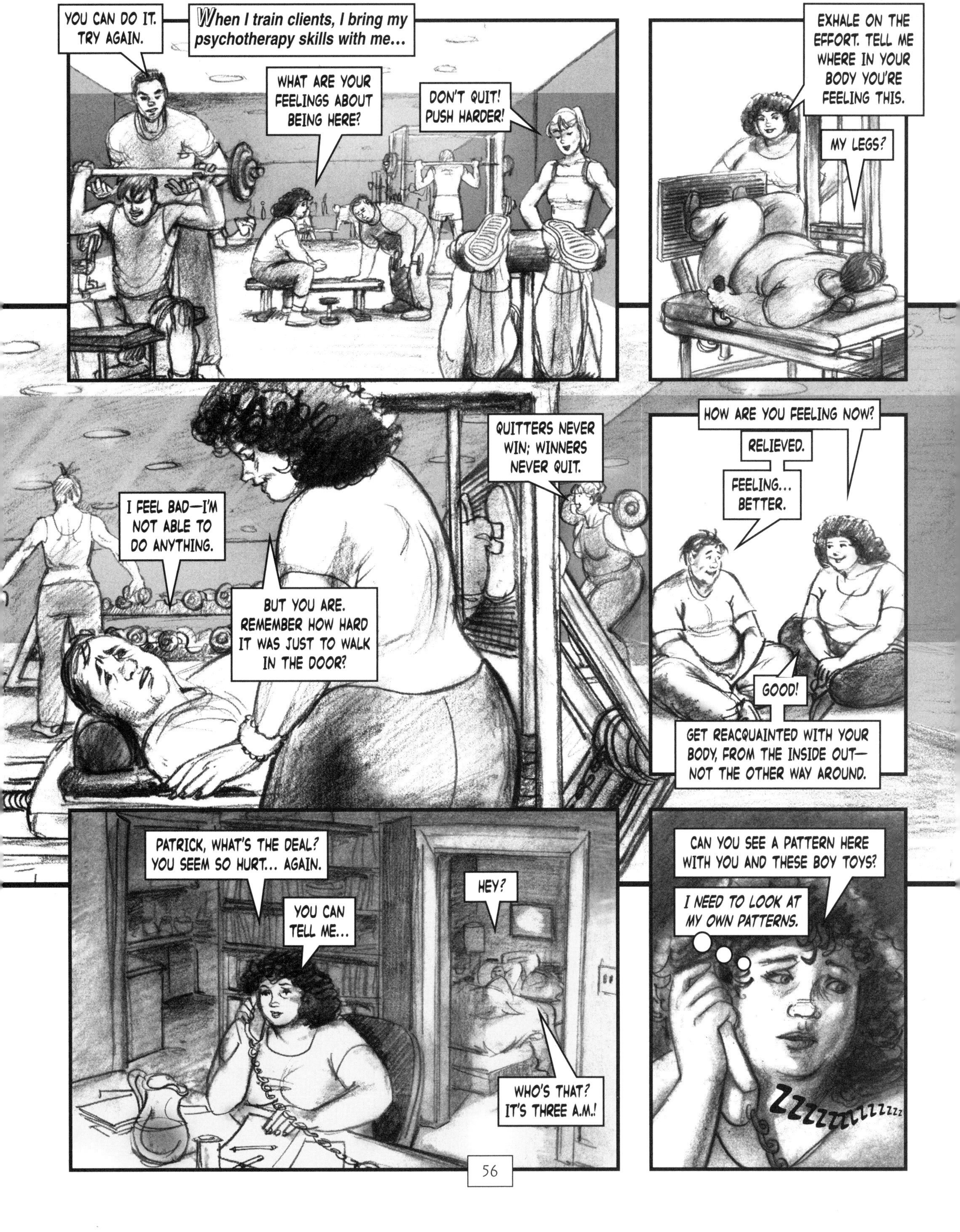
YOU CAN DO IT. TRY AGAIN.
When I train clients, I bring my psychotherapy skills with me…
WHAT ARE YOUR FEELINGS ABOUT BEING HERE?
DON'T QUIT! PUSH HARDER!
EXHALE ON THE EFFORT. TELL ME WHERE IN YOUR BODY YOU'RE FEELING THIS.
MY LEGS?
I FEEL BAD—I'M NOT ABLE TO DO ANYTHING.
BUT YOU ARE. REMEMBER HOW HARD IT WAS JUST TO WALK IN THE DOOR?
QUITTERS NEVER WIN; WINNERS NEVER QUIT.
HOW ARE YOU FEELING NOW?
RELIEVED.
FEELING… BETTER.
GOOD!
GET REACQUAINTED WITH YOUR BODY, FROM THE INSIDE OUT—NOT THE OTHER WAY AROUND.
PATRICK, WHAT'S THE DEAL? YOU SEEM SO HURT… AGAIN.
YOU CAN TELL ME…
HEY?
WHO'S THAT? IT'S THREE A.M.!
CAN YOU SEE A PATTERN HERE WITH YOU AND THESE BOY TOYS?
I NEED TO LOOK AT MY OWN PATTERNS.
ZZZZZZZZZZZzzz

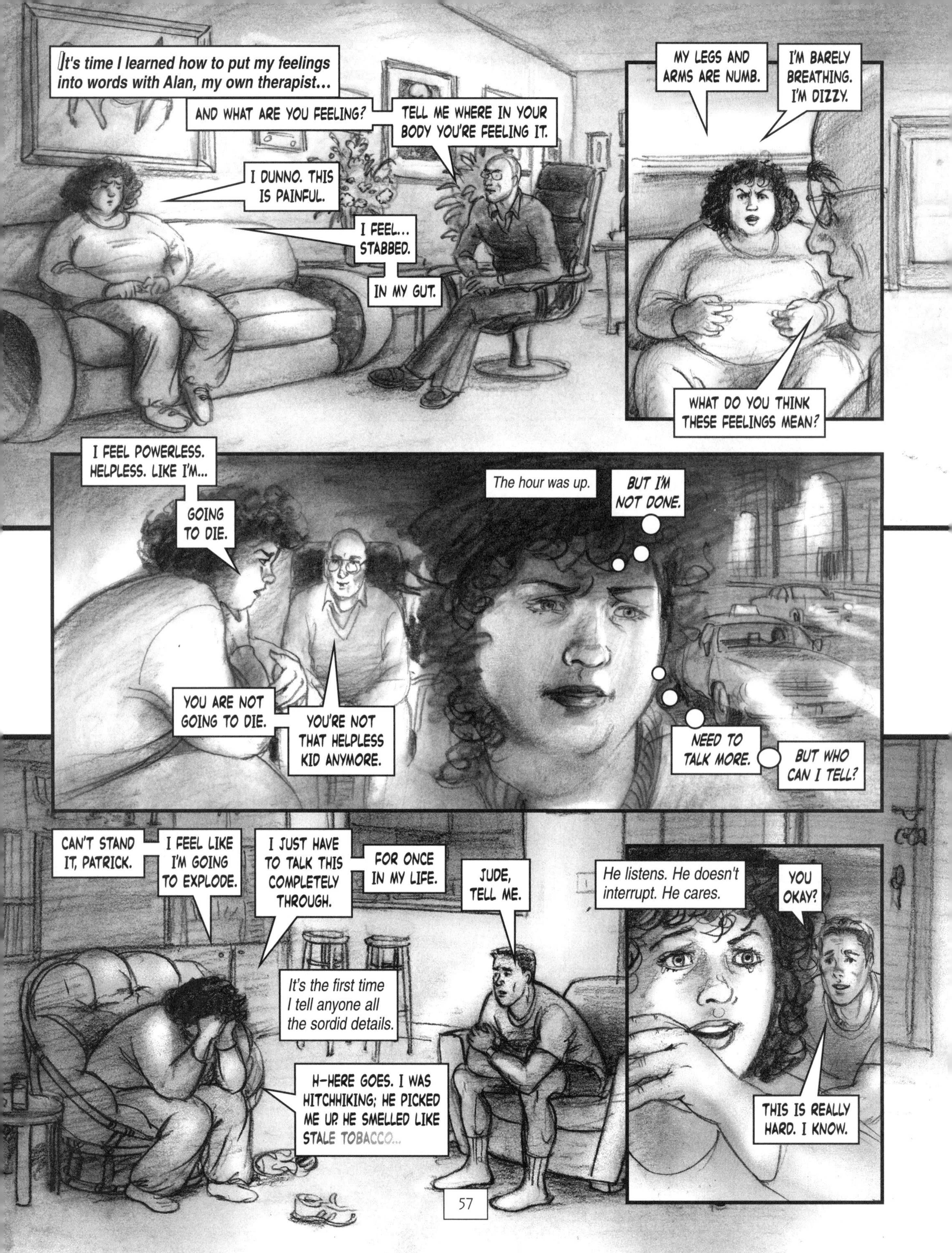

It's time I learned how to put my feelings into words with Alan, my own therapist...
AND WHAT ARE YOU FEELING?
TELL ME WHERE IN YOUR BODY YOU'RE FEELING IT.
I DUNNO. THIS IS PAINFUL.
I FEEL... STABBED.
IN MY GUT.
MY LEGS AND ARMS ARE NUMB.
I'M BARELY BREATHING. I'M DIZZY.
WHAT DO YOU THINK THESE FEELINGS MEAN?
I FEEL POWERLESS. HELPLESS. LIKE I'M...
GOING TO DIE.
YOU ARE NOT GOING TO DIE.
YOU'RE NOT THAT HELPLESS KID ANYMORE.
The hour was up.
BUT I'M NOT DONE.
NEED TO TALK MORE.
BUT WHO CAN I TELL?
CAN'T STAND IT, PATRICK.
I FEEL LIKE I'M GOING TO EXPLODE.
I JUST HAVE TO TALK THIS COMPLETELY THROUGH.
FOR ONCE IN MY LIFE.
JUDE, TELL ME.
It's the first time I tell anyone all the sordid details.
H-HERE GOES. I WAS HITCHHIKING; HE PICKED ME UP. HE SMELLED LIKE STALE TOBACCO...
He listens. He doesn't interrupt. He cares.
YOU OKAY?
THIS IS REALLY HARD. I KNOW.

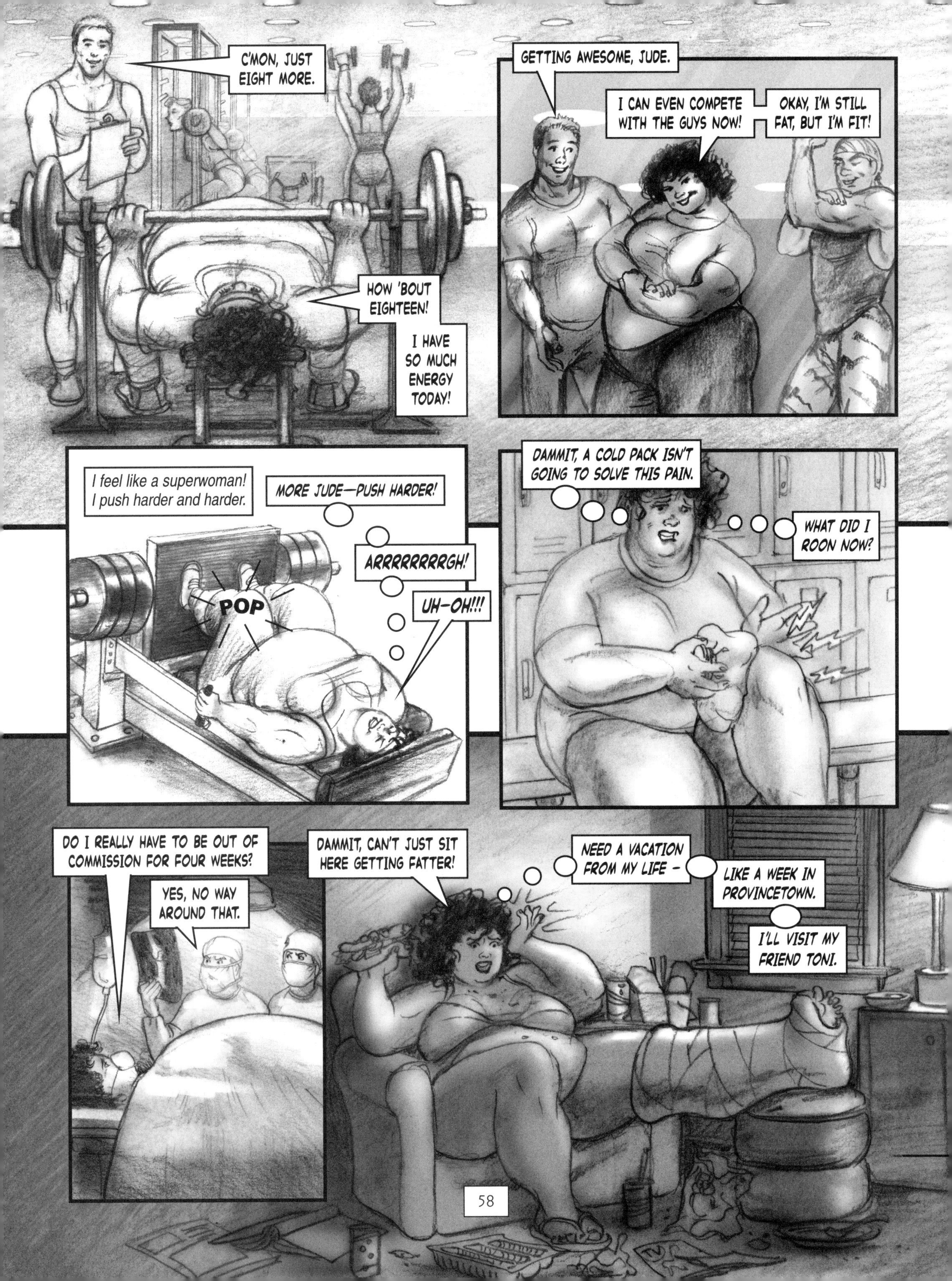
C'MON, JUST EIGHT MORE.
HOW 'BOUT EIGHTEEN!
I HAVE SO MUCH ENERGY TODAY!
GETTING AWESOME, JUDE.
I CAN EVEN COMPETE WITH THE GUYS NOW!
OKAY, I'M STILL FAT, BUT I'M FIT!
I feel like a superwoman! I push harder and harder.
MORE JUDE—PUSH HARDER!
ARRRRRRRRGH!
POP
UH-OH!!!
DAMMIT, A COLD PACK ISN'T GOING TO SOLVE THIS PAIN.
WHAT DID I ROON NOW?
DO I REALLY HAVE TO BE OUT OF COMMISSION FOR FOUR WEEKS?
YES, NO WAY AROUND THAT.
DAMMIT, CAN'T JUST SIT HERE GETTING FATTER!
NEED A VACATION FROM MY LIFE –
LIKE A WEEK IN PROVINCETOWN.
I'LL VISIT MY FRIEND TONI.

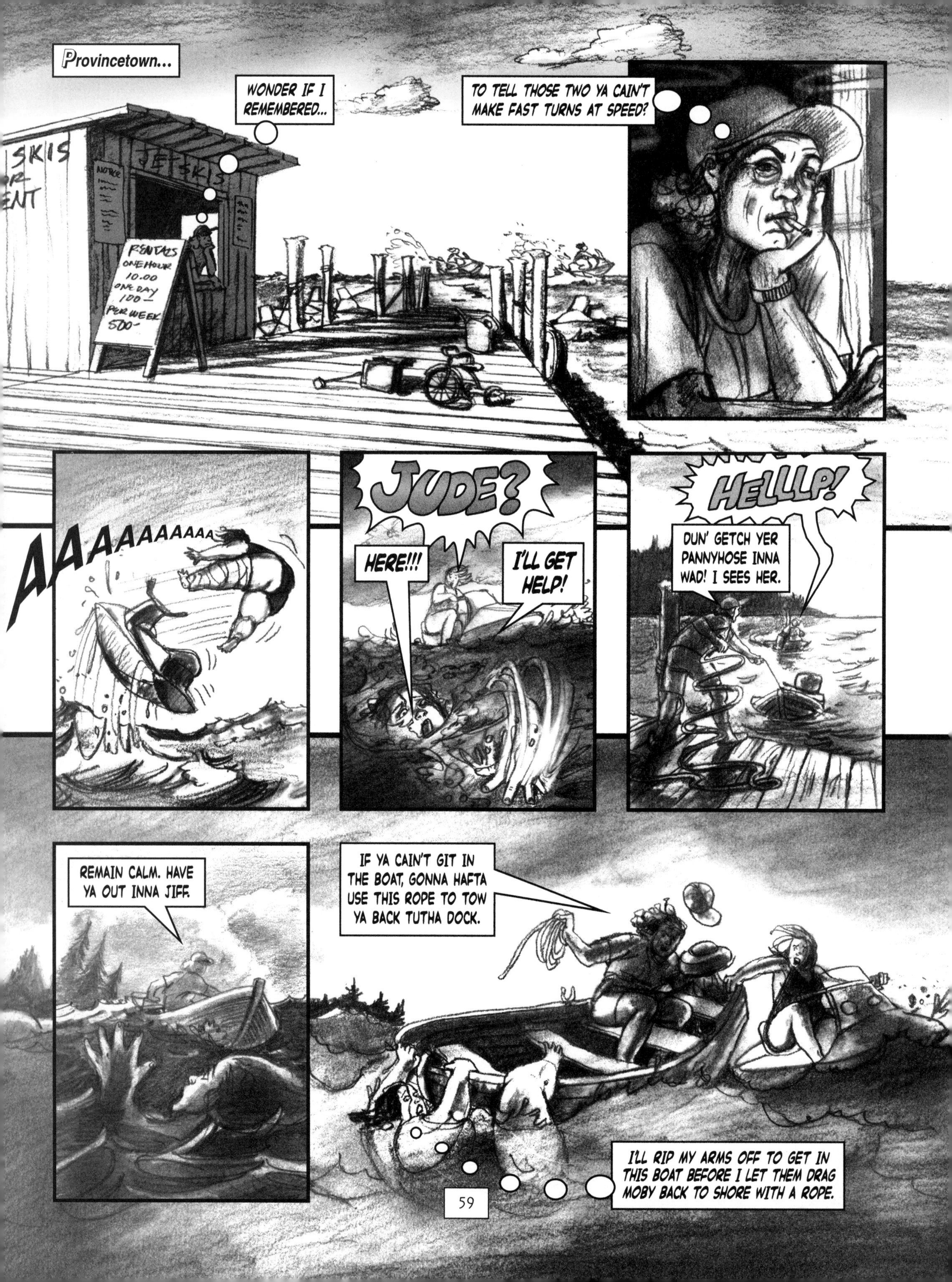
Provincetown...
WONDER IF I REMEMBERED...
TO TELL THOSE TWO YA CAIN'T MAKE FAST TURNS AT SPEED?
RENTALS ONE HOUR 10.00 ONE DAY 100— PER WEEK 500—
JETSKIS
AAAAAAAAAA
JUDE?
HERE!!!
I'LL GET HELP!
HELLLP!
DUN' GETCH YER PANNYHOSE INNA WAD! I SEES HER.
REMAIN CALM. HAVE YA OUT INNA JIFF.
IF YA CAIN'T GIT IN THE BOAT, GONNA HAFTA USE THIS ROPE TO TOW YA BACK TUTHA DOCK.
I'LL RIP MY ARMS OFF TO GET IN THIS BOAT BEFORE I LET THEM DRAG MOBY BACK TO SHORE WITH A ROPE.

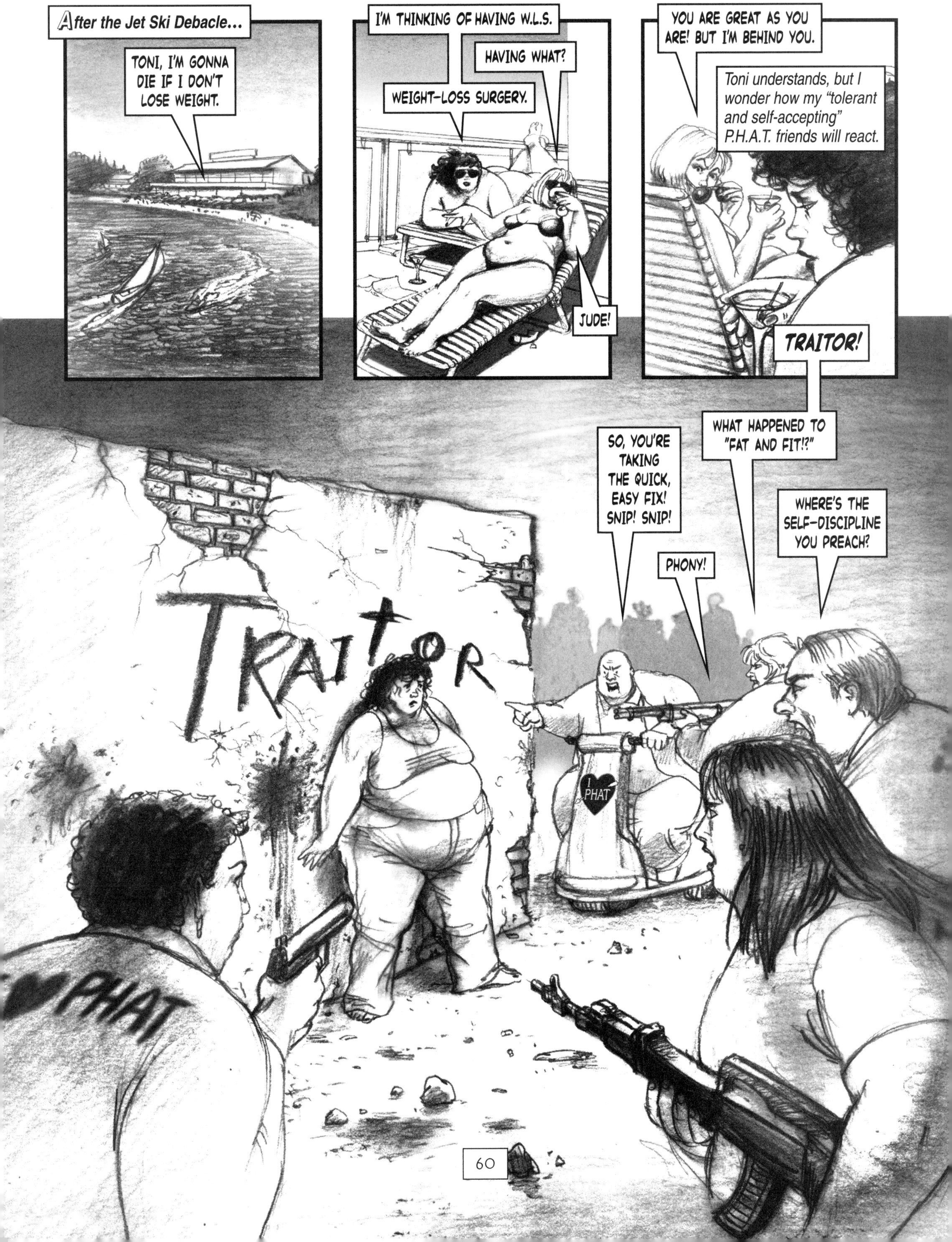
After the Jet Ski Debacle...
TONI, I'M GONNA DIE IF I DON'T LOSE WEIGHT.
I'M THINKING OF HAVING W.L.S.
HAVING WHAT?
WEIGHT-LOSS SURGERY.
JUDE!
YOU ARE GREAT AS YOU ARE! BUT I'M BEHIND YOU.
Toni understands, but I wonder how my "tolerant and self-accepting" P.H.A.T. friends will react.
TRAITOR!
WHAT HAPPENED TO "FAT AND FIT!?"
SO, YOU'RE TAKING THE QUICK, EASY FIX! SNIP! SNIP!
WHERE'S THE SELF-DISCIPLINE YOU PREACH?
PHONY!
TRAITOR
I PHAT
PHAT

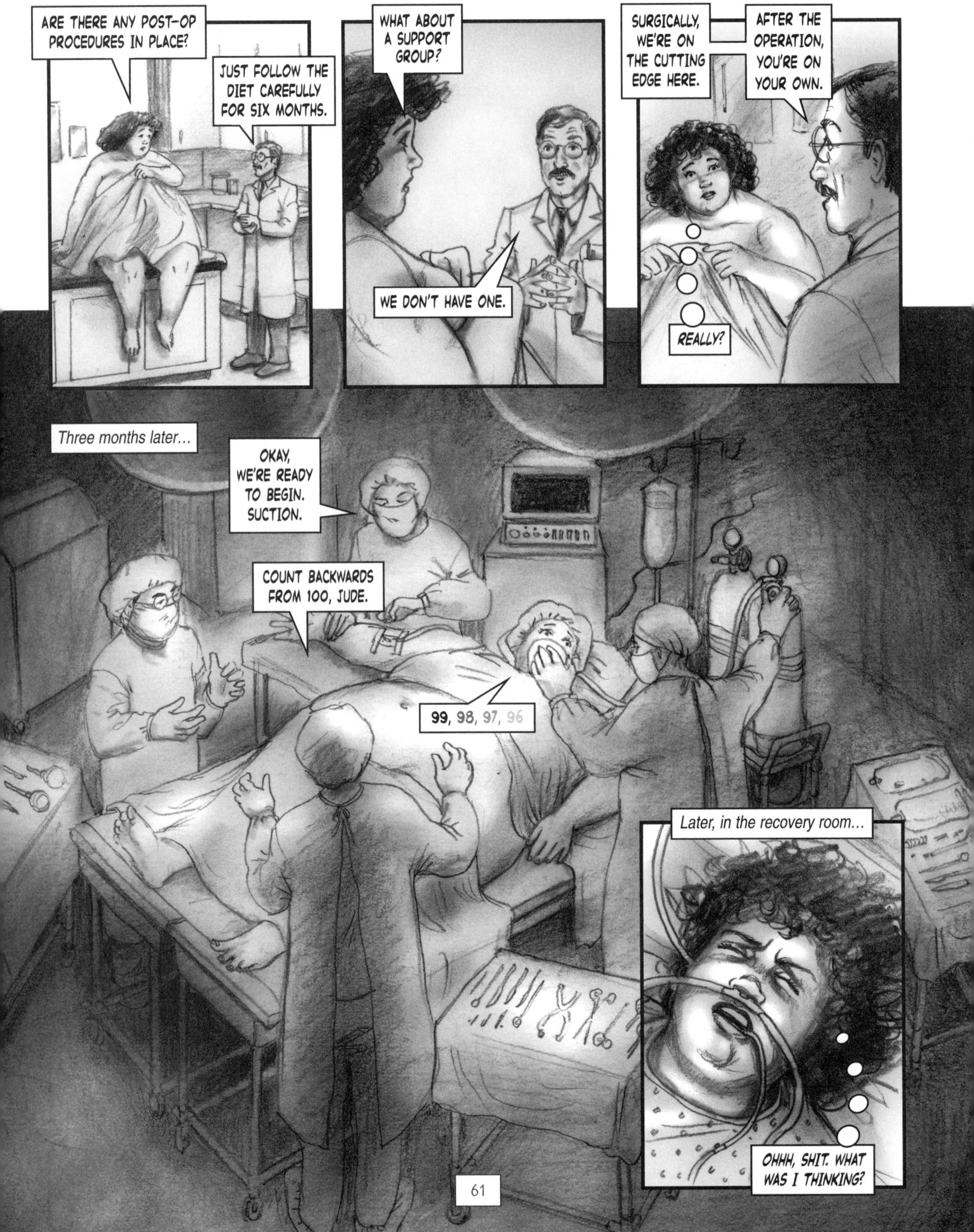
ARE THERE ANY POST-OP PROCEDURES IN PLACE?
JUST FOLLOW THE DIET CAREFULLY FOR SIX MONTHS.
WHAT ABOUT A SUPPORT GROUP?
WE DON'T HAVE ONE.
SURGICALLY, WE'RE ON THE CUTTING EDGE HERE.
AFTER THE OPERATION, YOU'RE ON YOUR OWN.
REALLY?
Three months later...
OKAY, WE'RE READY TO BEGIN. SUCTION.
COUNT BACKWARDS FROM 100, JUDE.
99, 98, 97, 96
Later, in the recovery room...
OHHH, SHIT. WHAT WAS I THINKING?

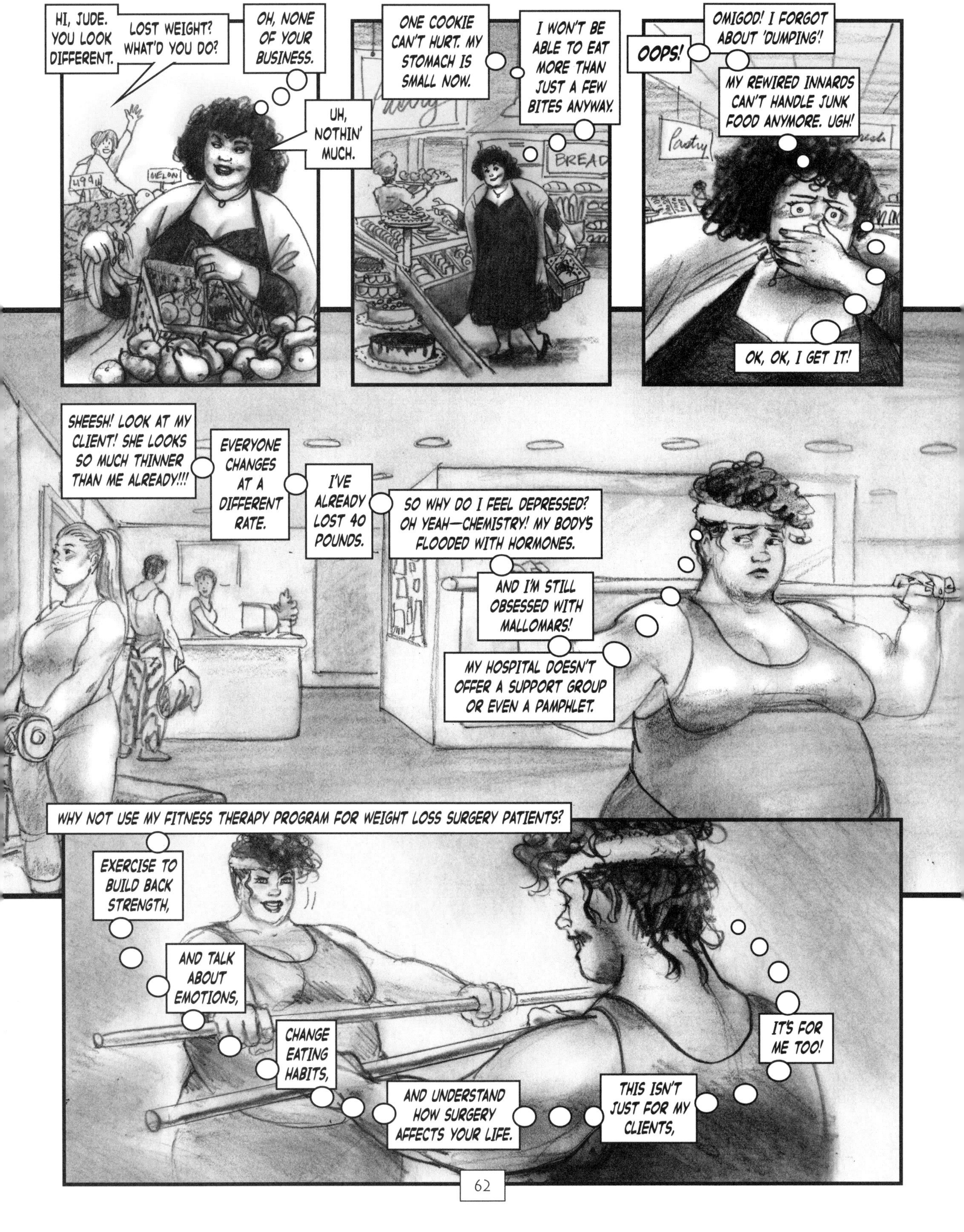
HI, JUDE. YOU LOOK DIFFERENT.
LOST WEIGHT? WHAT'D YOU DO?
OH, NONE OF YOUR BUSINESS.
UH, NOTHIN' MUCH.
ONE COOKIE CAN'T HURT. MY STOMACH IS SMALL NOW.
I WON'T BE ABLE TO EAT MORE THAN JUST A FEW BITES ANYWAY.
BREAD
OOPS!
OMIGOD! I FORGOT ABOUT 'DUMPING'!
MY REWIRED INNARDS CAN'T HANDLE JUNK FOOD ANYMORE. UGH!
Pastry
OK, OK, I GET IT!
SHEESH! LOOK AT MY CLIENT! SHE LOOKS SO MUCH THINNER THAN ME ALREADY!!!
EVERYONE CHANGES AT A DIFFERENT RATE.
I'VE ALREADY LOST 40 POUNDS.
SO WHY DO I FEEL DEPRESSED? OH YEAH—CHEMISTRY! MY BODY'S FLOODED WITH HORMONES.
AND I'M STILL OBSESSED WITH MALLOMARS!
MY HOSPITAL DOESN'T OFFER A SUPPORT GROUP OR EVEN A PAMPHLET.
WHY NOT USE MY FITNESS THERAPY PROGRAM FOR WEIGHT LOSS SURGERY PATIENTS?
EXERCISE TO BUILD BACK STRENGTH,
AND TALK ABOUT EMOTIONS,
CHANGE EATING HABITS,
AND UNDERSTAND HOW SURGERY AFFECTS YOUR LIFE.
THIS ISN'T JUST FOR MY CLIENTS,
IT'S FOR ME TOO!

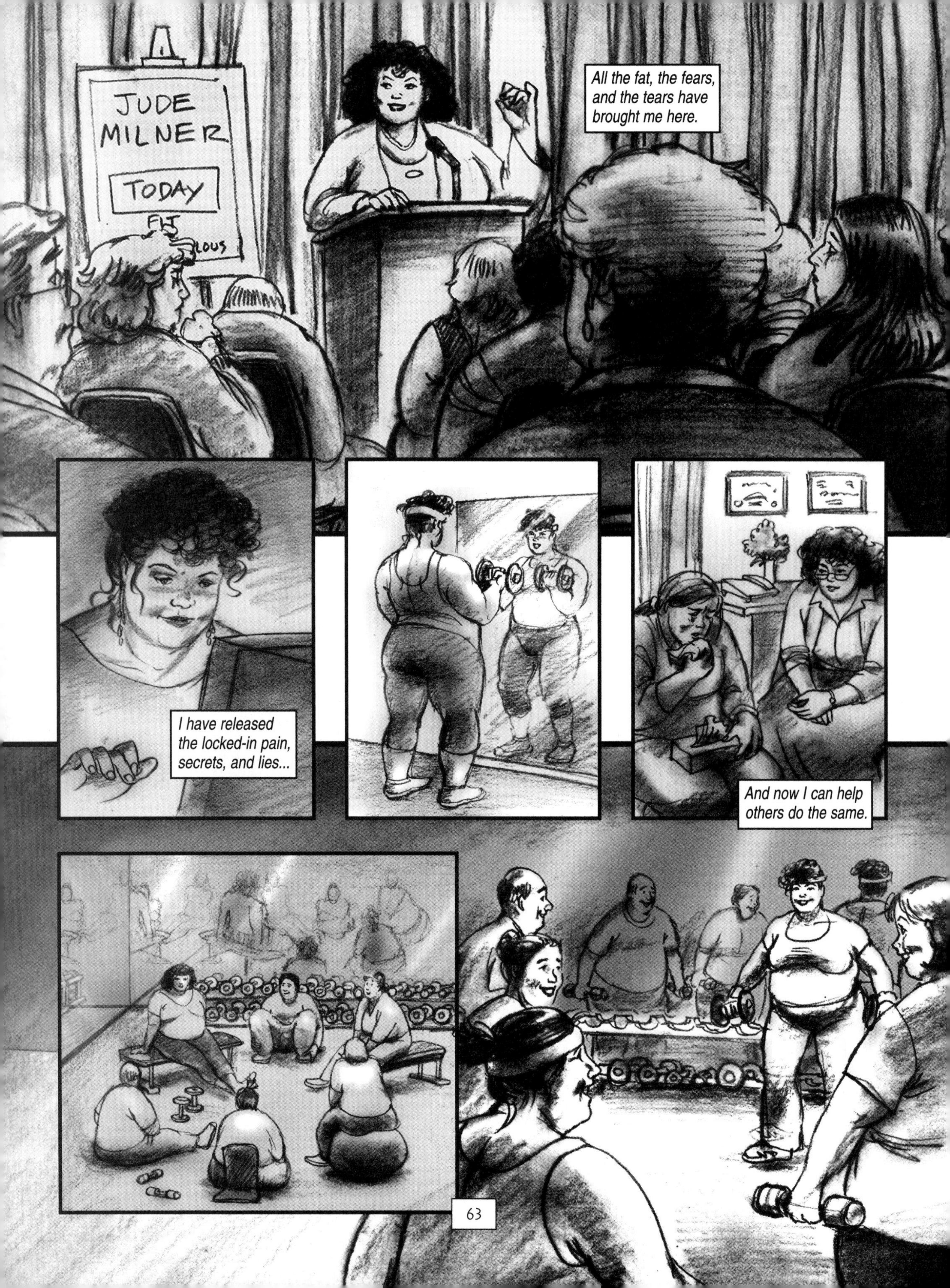
JUDE
MILNER
TODAY
All the fat, the fears, and the tears have brought me here.
I have released the locked-in pain, secrets, and lies...
And now I can help others do the same.

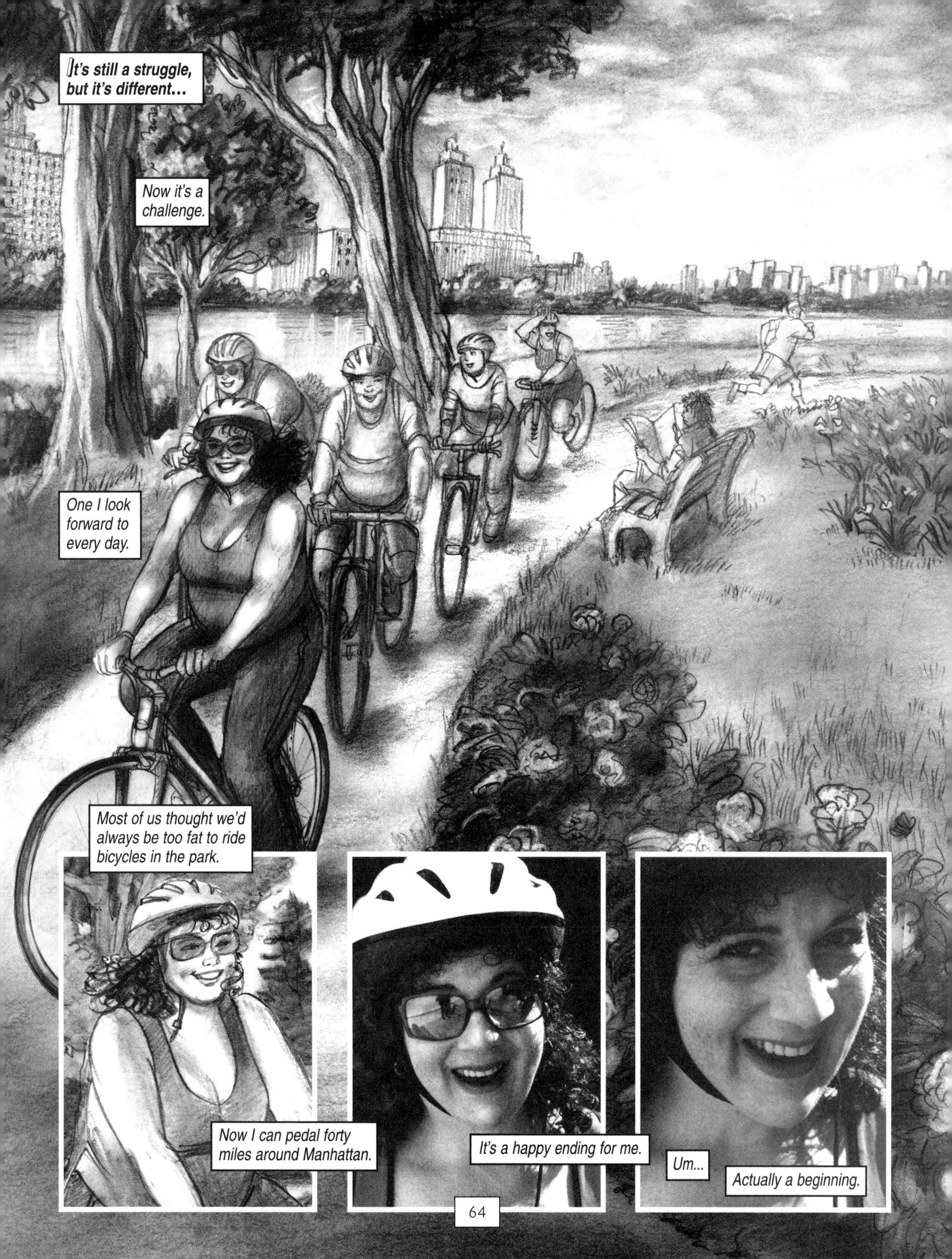
It's still a struggle, but it's different...
Now it's a challenge.
One I look forward to every day.
Most of us thought we'd always be too fat to ride bicycles in the park.
Now I can pedal forty miles around Manhattan.
It's a happy ending for me.
Um...
Actually a beginning.

JUDE MILNER, a licensed psychotherapist and certified fitness trainer with a private practice in New York City, is a pioneer in developing crucial support and recuperative programs for obese patients. This autobiography is her first book. Visit Jude's website at www.fitnesstherapy.org.

MARY WILSHIRE (illustrator) obtained a degree in painting from the Pratt Institute, and has bounced between the worlds of editorial illustration, comics, advertising, and fine art for thirty years. Her work for Marvel Comics includes the series *Power Pack*, *Red Sonja*, *Spider-Man*, and *Barbie*. She lives in Westchester County, New York, with her husband and their two daughters.

RICHARD MILNER (producer and script writer) is an anthropologist, historian, and the author of *The Encyclopedia of Evolution: Humanity's Quest for Its Origins*. A senior editor at *Natural History Magazine* at the American Museum of Natural History, he often appears on the History Channel, A & E *Biographies*, *Nova*, and *Animal Planet*. He lives in New York City, and performs his one-man show *Charles Darwin: Live & In Concert* all over the world.

JAMES SHERMAN (designer and art director) began as a political cartoonist for the *Bergen Record*, and now focuses on design and art direction for movies, television, music videos, books, magazines, and online media. He lives in New York City.